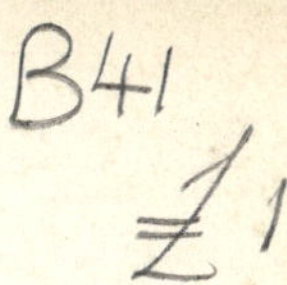

THE WAR IN THE AIR 1914—1918

JACK WOODHOUSE and

G. A. EMBLETON

ALMARK PUBLISHING CO. LTD., LONDON.

W.A.—1

First Published—1974

ISBN O 85524 179 9 (Hard cover edition)
ISBN O 85524 178 0 (Paper cover edition)

Printed in Great Britain by
Chapel River Press, Andover, Hants., SP10 3 NS
For the Publishers, Almark Publishing Co. Ltd.,
49 Malden Way, New Malden,
Surrey, KT3 6EA, England.

CONTENTS

The authors and publishers wish to thank the Imperial War Museum for their invaluable help in supplying most of the photographs featured in this book.

INTRODUCTION

THE Wright Brothers first experimented with methods of controlling aircraft, using gliders, from 1900 to 1902. Then they built their own engine and on 17th. December, 1903 made the world's first powered, sustained, and controlled flight. It lasted 12 seconds.

In England, the news was regarded as fantastic and in many quarters it was seriously discussed whether the flight was genuine or a fake. During a debate in Parliament a minister scorned the idea that the aeroplane could have a serious part to play in war or peace, relegating it to the level of a leisure-time sporting activity. The only serious opposition to this reactionary outlook came from a young man named Winston Churchill.

In 1905, the improved third version of the Wright Flyer became the first practical aeroplane in history which could stay in the air for half an hour and be manoeuvred under the full control of the pilot.

In Europe, little was known of the Wright Brothers' achievements and little or no technical benefit was derived from them. It was principally in France that original lines of thought were followed but the first flight there was not achieved until 1906. The machine however, was of an entirely different type from that of the Wrights.

From that time onwards development was continuous. In 1909 Bleriot flew the Channel in his Type XI to win the Daily Mail £1000 prize. Up to 1914, and early in the Great War, the Type XI was used in large numbers by the British and French as a training and reconnaissance aircraft.

Although trials were made with aircraft for military use before 1914, the British General Staff were not impressed with their likely usefulness and importance as weapons of war. They considered cavalry to be more effective for reconnaissance and certainly more acceptable than the noisy aeroplanes, which frightened the horses.

The Germans had been much more receptive to new ideas and by 1914 had trained artillery observation units using balloons, and infantry units to advance in co-operation with reconnaissance reports from aeroplanes.

The use of aeroplanes for reconnaissance led to the use by the other side of armed aeroplanes to attack the reconnoitring intruder before he could return with the information he had gathered—this was often passed back by dropping message bags. At first, revolvers and rifles were used, but soon purpose-built fighters were developed.

It was not long before it occurred to some fighter pilots that it would be a good idea, while cruising over a target, to drop something nasty on it, rather than to return to base with a map reference and call up the artillery to bombard it. So hand-held, 'over the side' bombing came into use, followed later by larger bombs suspended on racks under the wings.

As early as 30th. August, 1914, the Germans began dropping two or three bombs (by hand) from an aeroplane flown over Paris every night at 6.00 p.m. These were the first bombs to be dropped on a city. On the second night the Parisians introduced a black-out.

In Russia, Igor Sikorsky built the World's first four-engined aircraft in 1913. This was followed by a four-engined bomber which by 1917 was carrying 1000 lbs of bombs.

THE WARRIORS TAKE TO THE AIR

British Military Beginnings

THE atmosphere in which aviation developed before 1914 is usually forgotten. The country was still in a state of euphoria arising from the Pax Britannica which had reached its culmination on Victoria's Diamond Jubilee, and the strength of its two-power Navy (the British Navy was twice as strong as that of any other country). The idea that any other country could threaten the all-powerful British Empire was inconceivable.

The Royal Engineers Balloon Company and the Balloon Factory at Farnborough were producing War Kites up to 1907, and an airship was also made there. In 1908 the manufacture of an aeroplane was begun and this flew in 1909. In the same year, the Army bought a Wright Biplane from the Hon. C. S. Rolls (the Rolls of Rolls-Royce).

The Short Brothers began to build aeroplanes in 1908 and were soon followed by others, including Handley Page, Bristol, Sopwith and A. V. Roe. The latter made the first flight of a British aircraft with a British engine, on 13th. July, 1909, in his little triplane with 9 h.p. J.A.P. engine over Lea Marshes, finishing in the river.

In 1911 the Air Battalion, Royal Engineers, was formed to operate five aeroplanes and one or two small, experimental airships. The Aeroplane Section was stationed at Larkhill on Salisbury Plain. Farman, Bleriot, and Nieuport aeroplanes were purchased from France, but no encouragement was given to any British constructor.

The Balloon Factory became the Army Aircraft Factory in 1911, acquiring the title of the Royal Aircraft Factory in 1912. Although this was set up as an experimental workshop, its considerable growth before the war led to the belief that it was intended to build all military aircraft there. The obvious intention was for Farnborough to become the centre of military aircraft design and production, with the private companies employed in the lesser role of sub-contractors.

This was an affront to the pioneers whose efforts had already contributed a great deal to the progress of aviation in this country. The Bristol Box Kite was in use as a training aircraft at private schools and Shorts had built the world's first twin-engined aircraft.

The Royal Flying Corps was formed from the Air Battalion in 1912, with Military and Navy Wings. The War Office pursued its policy of obtaining its aircraft from the Royal Aircraft Factory and before the war decided to standardise on the BE.2c. It was designed by Geoffrey de Havilland while he was employed at the Factory and was a good aeroplane for its time. However, the Admiralty decided not to standardise but to buy the best aircraft available, whether made by the Factory or private industry.

Very few aeroplanes were purchased by the War Office except on one remarkable occasion in 1913 when an M.P. challenged the War Secretary to tell the House of Commons how many aeroplanes the Army had. A number in excess of 100 was given in reply. The M.P. disputed this and insisted on counting them and made the total 13. Within a few days the Government purchased any reasonable aeroplane they could in order to make up the quantity.

The establishment of the R.F.C. at that time was: 7 Squadrons each of 12 aircraft and 12 pilots; plus a reserve of 12 aircraft and 12 pilots per squadron.

This made a total establishment of 168 aircraft with pilots but these figures were not reached before the outbreak of war. By the Autumn of 1913 when the Army Manoeuvres were held, only about 50 aircraft could be assembled.

When the war came in August 1914, the R.F.C. Squadrons were equipped with a variety of aircraft, including a number of French types, but Factory-designed BE.2as and BE.2bs predominated. The BE.2c was not delivered to squadrons until later in the year. All the engines in use by the R.F.C. at this time were foreign, mainly French.

Serny Aerodrome, 17th. June 1918.

Pilots and Observers of 22 Squadron handing over papers, etc., before going on patrol, in accordance with the notice 'Empty your pockets before going on patrol'. This precaution was taken to prevent information reaching the enemy in the event of a forced landing. In the background are some of the Bristol Fighters of the squadron.

The Birth of French Military Aviation

The motor car and internal combustion engine were enthusiastically received and developed in France from the very beginning, before the turn of the century. There were no harsh restrictions on road vehicles, such as those which hampered them in England.

As a result the French were supplying complete cars and motor cycles to England and the continental countries from these early days and from 1900 onwards were also supplying most of the engines to be fitted in the vehicles made in those countries. Thus a strong automobile and engine industry was built up. In due course this provided the expertise and manufacturing capability for the important aero engine and airframe industry which became second to none in Europe.

The potential of military aviation was also recognised early and was encouraged. Prior to 1910 the only official establishment consisted of four Balloon Sections, but a number of soldiers and officers gained experience privately as pilots.

The first Military Aviation Unit was formed early in 1910. The Picardy Aerial Manoeuvres carried out later in the year showed the future promise of the aeroplane in war. Like the British, the French foresaw the usefulness of the aeroplane for reconnaissance but saw further, that the aeroplane could supersede the cavalry (they may well have been assisted to this conclusion by the experiences with the use of aeroplanes for reconnaissance in the troubles in Algeria and Morocco between 1912 and 1914).

In 1911 Regional Flying Schools were set up. There were trials of co-operation with the artillery and the cavalry, and in the Grand Manoeuvres of that year the value of the aeroplane for army co-operation work was confirmed. A Military Competition was held for which the machines had to meet stiff technical and performance requirements.

Although there was not yet an official aviation corps, flying operations were organised by Escadrilles (roughly equivalent to a Squadron). These were given a certain amount of autonomy and formed a sound basis for later expansion.

By the end of 1911 there were 120 pilots and pupils in training. At the end of 1912 the number had swelled to 250. The requirements for a Military Aviation Certificate were tightened up at this time; they included covering a triangular course of some 120 miles in two or more flights, two flights of about 90 miles in a straight line and 45 minutes at not less than 2500 feet. Michelin, the tyre manufacturer, put up a handsome prize for a bomb dropping competition.

In 1912 an Aviation Corps was formed in three Groups. The manufacture and purchase of engines and aeroplanes for the Aviation Service was concentrated in the S.F.A. (Service des Fabrications de l'Aeronautique) at Chalais Meudon. This was an almost exact counterpart of the Royal Aircraft Factory at Farnborough. It was to have an equally harmful effect on the French Service d'Aviation Militaire until it was reformed towards the end of 1917.

When the war began, there were, ready and equipped: 21 Squadrons, each with 6 two-seaters for Army co-operation, and 4 units, each with 3 Bleriots for liaison with the Cavalry.

How the Germans Began

The first practical controlled flight of a power driven aircraft in Germany was made by the large, rigid Zeppelin LZ.1 on 2nd. July, 1900, over Lake Constance. Development continued but LZ.1 was scrapped due to lack of funds early in 1901, and LZ.2 was destroyed in a storm following its second test flight in January 1906.

Early in 1906 the German War Ministry held conferences with the General Staff to consider the future development of military aviation. Their views were influenced by the performance of the airship up to that time. It appeared much more promising than the aeroplane and seemed likely to become useful for military purposes.

For his part, Count Zeppelin envisaged his large, rigid airships being used rather like battleships, making sorties from, and returning to, a base at the rear of operations.

But the Army specialists wanted an aerial vehicle, under their direct control. They thought of the airship as a balloon which they already had in service and which was transported to the scene of operations, inflated on the spot and used from forward bases. Accordingly, for Army support purposes they decided to carry out experiments with smaller, semi-rigid and non-rigid types.

There was already in existence an Airship Battalion, and a Company within the Battalion constructed the first Army experimental, semi-rigid airship. It was followed by a second in 1907 and then in 1908 by the first (non-rigid) Parseval Airship.

In 1908 the General Staff formed a Technical Section especially to investigate the military applications of Wireless Telegraphy, Motor Transport and Aviation. They planned to have a fleet of 15 airships in service by 1910. Zeppelin's third airship was accepted by the Army in 1909 and commissioned as Z.1.

The resources devoted to airships made the War Ministry reluctant to spend additional money on experiments with aeroplanes. However, the insistence of the General Staff led to the War Ministry giving financial help to promising aeroplane constructors.

The Army still did not possess any aeroplanes in 1910, but a small, shoe-string unit was formed to train officer volunteer pilots. By early 1911 ten had been trained. Then a combined War Ministry and General Staff Commission looked into the aviation needs of the Army; this led to 30 aeroplanes being purchased. By the end of 1911, a total of 37 aeroplanes were available and 30 pilots had been trained.

During 1912 the Military Aviation Service was formed. The General Staff decided to maintain the fleet of rigid airships but to discontinue the use of the smaller and faster non-rigid and semi-rigid types intended for reconnaissance and army co-operation work. Instead, they decided to use aeroplanes. Flying training was put out under contract, to schools run by aircraft manufacturers who were making military aeroplanes.

In 1913, 120 monoplanes and 120 biplanes were bought. Aviation battalions were formed, each of 3 companies, plus a further battalion of 2 companies with the Bavarian Army. For 1914, four Aviation Battalions were planned, to be split up into 48 Field Aviation Units, each with 6 aeroplanes.

During the first part of 1914, pilot training was speeded up and aerial observers were also trained. Use of aircraft for reconnaissance was practised with regiments undergoing artillery training. Success was limited because of the lack of suitable means of communication with the artillery; wireless was not yet sufficiently portable and reliable. Experiments with bomb dropping and bomb sights were also carried out, but the results were not good enough to suggest any great use of aircraft for this purpose. Orders had been placed for the delivery, in 1914, of replacements for all the aircraft on the strength in 1913 and to build up to 1000 aeroplanes of standard monoplane and biplane types.

At the outbreak of war in August 1914, the following mobile units were ready:

8 Balloon Field Aviation Units, each with 2 balloons (one a reserve) and 1 kite balloon, and a Gas Transport Column to inflate the balloons.

15 Balloon Field Aviation Troops, each with 1 kite balloon and and several free balloons. These units were to protect fortress towns and military bases.

18 Airship detachments as crews for the 12 Army airships, which included 7 rigid Zeppelin types.

33 Field Aviation Units equipped with 6 aeroplanes each.

7 Fortress Aviation Units, each with 4 aeroplanes.

A year by year comparison of the British and German programmes shows how the German Government realised the importance of military aviation to a much greater degree.

THE WAR YEARS

1914

DURING the first months of the War, the Germans advanced almost to Paris before being stopped on the Marne, and then drove northward towards the Channel Ports. The British sent a Naval Division to Antwerp but it was not sufficiently strong to withstand the German onslaught. During the evacuation of Antwerp which followed early in October 1914, the small Naval Air Service Squadron made a last effort to bomb the Zeppelin sheds at Cologne and Dusseldorf while they were still within range. The attempt on Cologne was not successful, but Flight Lieutenant Marix bombed the Zeppelin Z.1X in its shed at Dusseldorf; it was completely destroyed. But Marix' Sopwith Tabloid was badly shot up by ground fire and he had to force-land 200 miles short of Antwerp. Borrowing a bicycle he reached base safely and in time for the general evacuation to Ostend.

The two-seaters were then the most important class of aeroplane, carrying out the duties of artillery spotting, reconnaissance, observation, contact patrol, photography and many jobs which needed an aerial maid-of-all-work to perform them. Without the two-seaters there would have been no need for the fighters.

Much of the front line between the opposing forces had stabilised by the end of October 1914 and the technique of artillery spotting soon developed, aided by the use of wireless. Originally, the reporting procedure was quite informal, but soon the 'Clock Code' method came into use. In this, the target was regarded as being at the centre of a large clock face, with 12 o'clock due north of the target, the other hours being in their usual positions round the clock. Imaginary circles drawn around the target as centre were given code letters, for example: 100 yards was B. So the information that the last shell had burst at a point 100 yards west of the target would be transmitted by Morse code simple as B9—9 o'clock being west of the target. Signals to the aircraft from the ground were made to a pre-arranged code by the use of white strips laid on the ground; this method was still used in the 1939 war and after.

Reconnaissance entailed flying over the enemy lines and behind them to look for new developments—building of fortifications and facilities, gathering of troops and supplies and so on.

Observation consisted of watching the progress of these developments and photography was used to record the situation for detailed analysis later.

Contact patrol was a valuable method of keeping in touch

Battle of the Marne, 1918. Bombardment in progress. German biplane patrolling the forward trenches and British tank in background.

with the progress of units during an advance, so that Head Quarters could be kept in touch with the battle and organise reinforcements and supplies.

1915

The harassment of the Allied reconnaissance aircraft by the Germans led to the conclusion that air fighting would soon become an important function. As there was no reliable method of firing bullets through the propeller disc of a tractor (or puller) aeroplane, the War Office decided to standardise on a two-seat pusher with a gunner in the nose. The Vickers FB.5 Gun Bus, built to this formula, went into Squadron service early in 1915 and was followed by the Factory's FE.2b.

The situation and resources of the Germans and Allied Forces led to quite different policies in the use of aircraft. The Allies had a numerical superiority of aircraft in the region of 30% and this led the Germans to be careful to avoid losses. This they achieved by doing a large part of their artillery spotting by balloon (which they hauled down rapidly when Allied aircraft were seen to be approaching) and by keeping their aircraft on their own side of the lines. Both sides protected their balloons with anti-aircraft guns.

The Allies on the other hand, pursued an offensive policy so that all their flying was done on the German side of the lines. This meant that the aircraft could come under ground fire twice in a mission. Both sides sent out fighters on offensive patrols—to look for and destroy the aircraft of the enemy. But while the Allies penetrated behind the German lines on such patrols, the Germans simply waited for them on their own side of the lines. As they could carry less petrol their speed and manoeuvreability were increased.

The Germans also scored because of their ability to put in the air new types of aeroplane in sufficient quantities to make a considerable impact. During 1915 the Germans built up a marked superiority in speed and performance with their single seater Fokker and Pfalz monoplanes over the British and French reconnaissance two-seaters in use at the time, and inflicted heavy losses on the Allies. These German monoplanes had originally been used as escorts for the German two-seaters but as a result of their success in harassing the Allies, other single seater biplanes were developed, including the Halberstadt D.II.

The 'secret weapon' they possessed was a machine gun firing straight ahead through the propeller disc, so the aircraft itself could be aimed at the target. Introduced by Anthony Fokker (a Dutchman who had established himself in Germany before the war) on his monoplanes, they were

Laying and loading an 18 pdr anti-aircraft gun on field carriage, Italian Front.

also fitted to the Pfalz and the Halberstadt D.II. An interrupter gear 'timed' the bullets to pass between the propeller blades. To protect the secret, German aircraft fitted with this gear were forbidden to cross the lines, lest an example should fall into Allied hands.

The Germans also began in 1915 to use Kampfeinsitzer Kommandos—K.E.K.—or Combat Single-Seater Commands. These were temporary groupings formed on the initiative of a few officers to operate as independent single-seater strike forces without being tied to escorting two-seaters. By the end of 1915 there were more than a hundred German single-seaters on the Western Front, many operating a K.E.K. and several German 'Aces' including Boelcke and Immelmann started their careers in this way.

It was from these K.E.K. that the first German fighter squadrons were later to be formed.

In the winter of 1915/16 these small monoplane fighters became known as the 'Fokker Scourge' or 'Fokker Menace' and began to drive the Allies from the sky. In Britain the result was a public outcry, and an attack was made in Parliament on the War Office policy of standardising on its factory-built aircraft for the R.F.C. The officials responsible for deciding which aircraft would be used were accused of having 'failed either by ignorance, intrigue or incompetence to provide the best machines that this country could produce' and thereby having sent British pilots to their death.

1916

The Royal Aircraft Factory was ordered to concentrate on research and development rather than on production even of prototypes. This shift of production to private industry was accompanied by some designers moving from the Factory; a notable example was Geoffrey de Havilland who joined the Aircraft Manufacturing Company. They built the DH.2 to his design and it proved to be the first British fighter able to meet the Germans on almost equal terms.

In preparation for the offensive against the great French Fortress of Verdun in February 1916, the Germans built up a large force and gained complete superiority in the air.

They had well over 100 single and two-seater aeroplanes in this section and the weight of numbers made their control of the air extend far behind the allied lines. Extensive bombing of railway junctions, roads and supply depots was carried out. This severely hampered the passage of

German camera in captive balloon.

Experimenting with Le Prieur rockets. These were invented by a French Naval Officer, to destroy Kit balloons or airships. They were attached to the interplane struts of an aeroplane and fired electrically. At best their range was less than 400 ft.

reinforcements and supplies to the front. German artillery observation aeroplanes worked relatively unhindered, ranging the guns. Among other targets, the forward French aerodromes were shelled, adding to the demoralising effect on Allied airmen.

Marshal Petain issued his famous Order of the Day calling for air superiority to be re-established. The Allies mustered their resources with a speed which surprised the Germans and the French managed to throw into the battle an even larger number of aircraft.

Included in the new French forces were six Fighter Escadrilles of Nieuport Bébé machines—the first modern fighter of the war. The commander of these fighters was Major de Rose who led them himself flying in formation. De Rose is credited with having been the first C.O. to employ fighter squadrons as units in action.

During the assault on Verdun the Germans were using up to 20 ballons on this section of the front, stationed 5 miles behind the lines, for artillery observation. Communications by telephone between the balloons and the ground and on to the artillery had been improved and the results were only too obvious to the French.

Accordingly, much effort was put into the provision of counter measures against balloons. In May 1916 when the French counter-attacked, a successful strike was made against the German balloons with electrically ignited rockets. Five balloons were shot down in flames.

The S.P.A.D. S.7 first came into service in the summer of 1916. It was smaller than its German counterparts, had a good rate of climb and was the fastest fighter at the Front from late 1916 to early 1917. Thought not so manoeuvreable as the rotary-engined types, it was very strong and could out-dive any German fighter. Many who tried to stay with it in a dive lost their wings. The S.P.A.D. 7 had one fixed gun synchronised to fire through the propeller.

It was followed by the S.P.A.D. 13 with 2 synchronised guns and a top speed of 130 m.p.h. This remained the standard French fighter to the end of the War.

During the period which led up to the first battle of the Somme in July 1916, the Allied strength in the air became almost three times that of the Germans. Moreover, the Allies now had fighters with a better performance than the Germans. This allowed the Allied bombers and observation aircraft to penetrate freely behind the German lines, thus reversing the position at the beginning of the year.

The Allies used 25 or so observation balloons on the Somme front and these were instrumental in knocking out many German guns. The fighters also attacked German balloons with success.

Both sides built up in numbers of aircraft and introduced new and improved types during the remainder of 1916, but air superiority remained in Allied hands.

At the end of 1916 the Germans reorganised their military aviation and formed a true Army Air Service.

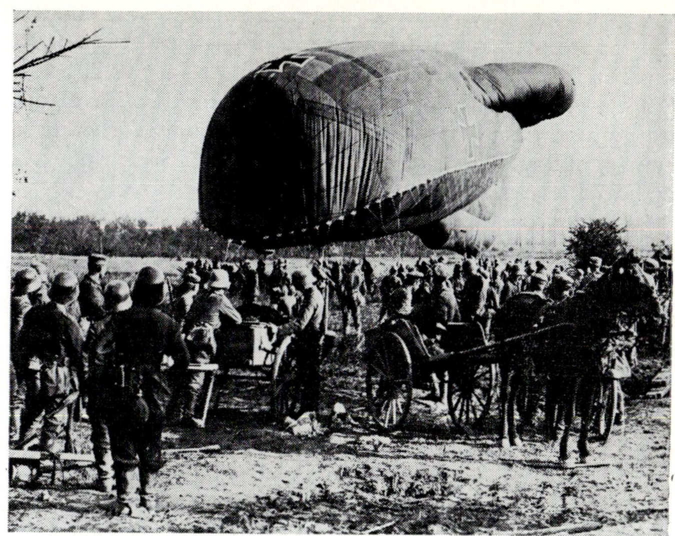

German observation balloon ready to ascend.

Command of the Flying Units passed from individual Corps Head Quarters to army G.H.Q.

1917

Towards the end of 1916 the Albatros D.1 fighters appeared on the Western Front. When the 1917 Spring offensives were opened, they slaughtered the obsolete BE.2 and RE.8 two-seaters of the R.F.C. engaged on observation, photography and artillery spotting duties. The heavy losses caused the worst month to be christened ‘Bloody April’.

The Germans developed the K.E.K. idea and adopted the use of independent fighter units or Jagdstaffel (Jasta for short). These were further grouped into Jagdgeschwader (J.G.)—a permanent grouping of four Jastas with a total strength of about 50 aeroplanes. 'Independent' means, of course, independent of Army control; in fact, the J.G. operated as a miniature Air Force.

There were four J.G. at this time and they were so successful that the Germans sought a way to cover the entire front, not just the vicinity of the J.G. station. The method adopted was to make up a special train to convey the complete J.G. with all their personnel, spares and equipment, from one area to another. With their brightly painted aircraft on flat trucks travelling with these special trains, the J.G. became known as 'Circuses'.

Hard pressed as they were in the Spring of 1917, the R.F.C. called to the Navy for help. From February to November eight Squadrons of R.N.A.S. Sopwith Triplanes were detached to operate with the R.F.C.—and with success, helped by their synchronised gun and astonishing manoeuvreability.

July 1917 saw the arrival of the Sopwith Camel—the first British fighter to have two machine guns firing through the propeller. Its manoeuvreability could be matched only by the Fokker Triplane, which suffered from being much slower.

A little later it was joined by the last design effort of the Royal Aircraft Factory, the SE.5. This had the 180 h.p., direct drive, Hispano Suiza engine. The SE.5a which followed it was to have had the 200 h.p., geared, Hispano Suiza engine, but difficulties with production of this engine led to most SE.5a's having the direct drive engine.

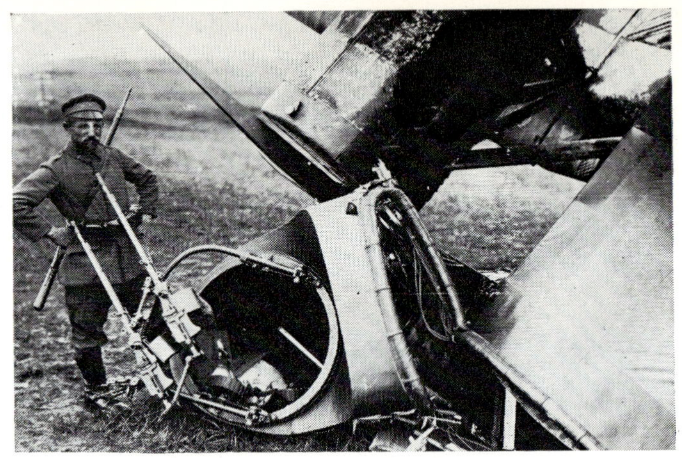

A British aeroplane shot down during September, 1918.

A new genre of aircraft appeared at this time, in both Britain and Germany. This was the two-seater fighter, well armed and fast enough to take care of itself and do battle with the single-seater fighter. Formation tactics allowed the rear gunners to protect each other's tails and foil this common method of attack by fighters. The Bristol Fighter FE.2b was a very fine aeroplane and remained in service for many years after the War. The German two-seater fighters were the Halberstadt CL.II and Hannoveraner CL.III which were also used in the ground attack role. This method of attack was coming into vogue in late 1917; not a little of its value was the boost to the morale of the ground

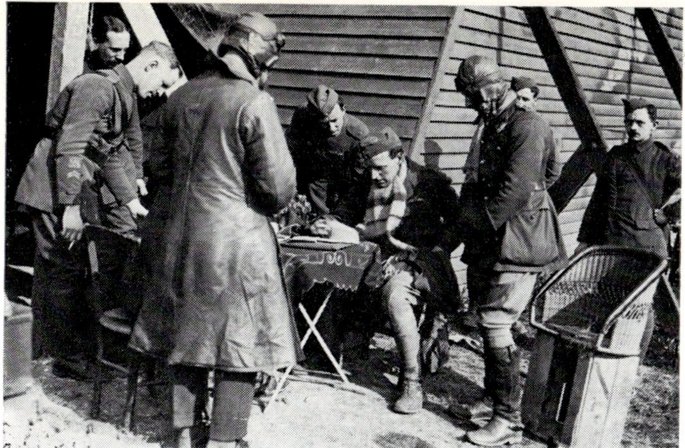

First Battle of Bapaume. The officer commanding 15th Squadron, Major H. V. Stammers, sits outside his office. Pilots hand in reports after flying over the enemy's lines, near Albert, 25th March, 1918.

troops when they saw their own aircraft going in over them. In September 1917, six CL.II squadrons caught all the reserves going up to a British Division in the line as they were crossing bridges over the Somme, causing great losses and confusion with repeated machine gun attacks and hand grenades.

1918

Although the United States entered the war in 1917, there was of course, a delay before the expected flow of material could become effective. The Germans considerably over-estimated the power of the U.S.A. to boost production quickly and made intensive preparations for the Great Battle of France. This was intended to break through the Allied defences, driving a wedge between the French and the British, to take the Channel ports and bring the War to an end before the expected massive supplies from America swung the balance against Germany.

Despite all the difficulties due to shortages of raw material and skilled labour, the number of German front line aircraft numbered nearly 3700 in March 1918. There were distributed among 81 Jastas of fighters, 38 ground attack units, 153 observation and reconnaissance units, and 7 bomber squadrons.

Approximately, half the fighters and bombers, a third of the ground attack units and two thirds of the reconnaissance units were to be held in reserve. The rest were secretly moved up to the forward areas ready for the battle.

On the first day, 21st. March, 1918, when the attack began, the Germans achieved an element of surprise—although the Allies had a good idea that an attack was coming, they did not know in what sector to expect it. The Jastas achieved complete mastery of the air and no Allied aircraft were able to cross the lines during the first two days. On the third day the Allies mustered their strength and were able to attack the German observation and ground support aircraft, and used low-flying aircraft to attack the advancing German infantry.

The momentum of the German advance ceased on 29th. March, having failed to drive between the British and French as planned. The German Army Air Service did not have a decisive effect on the battle. It might have done so if the available aircraft and pilots had been committed in a bold attack with greater numbers.

On the other hand, the Germans were short of day

bombers; they had been unable to increase the diversity of types to cover this need. A further problem, which had not been fully appreciated at the planning stage, was the difficulty of moving forward to suitable operational aerodromes with the advance. Destroyed Allied aerodromes, ruined roads and supply difficulties hampered the Air Service Units severely. There was a high wastage of aircraft; more than half of total losses were not attributable to enemy action.

The Germans had stepped up aircraft production in the first half of 1918 to 1100 per month and reached nearly 1500 in July 1918. But a new difficulty now appeared: there were nearly 2600 pilots at the front and between 300 and 400 replacements were needed each month. It was now realised that the training of pilots and observers could no longer keep pace with the demand.

In January 1918 an Air Ministry was set up in London for the supply of men and material under a Secetary of State for Air. Major General Trenchard was appointed Chief of the Air Staff. On 1st. April, 1918, the R.F.C. and R.N.A.S. were united to form the Royal Air Force. (To avoid confusion the Royal Aircraft Factory was re-christened the Royal Aircraft Establishment or R.A.E.).

In July of the same year the Independent Force of the R.A.F. was formed and began strategic bombing of industrial and communications targets in Germany. About 17,000 tons of bombs were dropped in 162 raids.

The Allies opened their offensive at Amiens on 8th. August with complete air superiority but after two or three days neither side could claim mastery. The German aces made high scores flying in their defensive role against the attacking Allies, downing 144 Allied aircraft in the first four days with the loss of 30 German aircraft.

The U.S. Army Air Service was commanded from August 1918 by Colonel Billy Mitchell. It was divided into Pursuit, Observation and Bombardment wings and was, perhaps, the first international air force. There were nearly 1500 aeroplanes and half of the 90 squadrons were French, while the Bombardment Wing included nine Squadrons of the R.A.F. Independent Air Force.

In the last two months of the war, air superiority again returned to the Allies and, together with Mitchell's command they attacked troops, trains, transport and supply dumps in support of the final Allied offensive.

THE AIRCRAFT

Aero Engines

As early as 1910 there were seventy firms making aero engines in mainland Europe. All types of engine were being built—rotary (crankshaft stationary, cylinders revolving), in-line and Vee, air cooled and water cooled.

Britain, on the other hand, lagged far behind. At the Fifth Aero Show, held at Olympia early in 1914, only seven British firms exhibited aero engines. With only one exception they were heavy water cooled in-line or Vee types—that is to say, heavy for the power produced per pound weight giving a high specific weight. For these engines the specific weight was 5 lb B.h.p. for the best to 10 lb B.h.p. for the worst; although the whole point of water cooling was to eliminate hot spots and distortion troubles, these water cooled engines did not produce any more power than their French air cooled rivals, or have a better life between overhauls.

The German water cooled in-line engines were better, with specific weights in 1914 between 4 and 4·4 lb/B.h.p. In most instances the figures quoted for the water cooled engines of any nationality do not include the radiators, plumbing or water, so the real figure is probably worse.

The French rotaries powered practically all the fastest aircraft from 1910 onwards until well into the War, with specific weights of 2·7 to 3·1 lb/B.h.p. Again, these figures are not entirely realistic, because these engines used much more petrol and oil for the power developed compared with the water cooled engines. For fighters with a limited duration, this was not so important as the light weight of the engines themselves.

In 1910 and in 1914 the British Government had tried to arouse interest among manufacturers by offering prizes in competitions for aero engines. £1000 was offered in 1910 as first prize, and £5000 in 1914. Gustavus Green won on both occasions but his engines, though reliable were heavy and did not go into production for war aircraft.

It is impossible to say, some 50 or 60 years later, whether it was fair to blame the British aero engine manufacturers for 'lack of interest', but fair or not, this was the case. It may be that the awards in the 1914 competition, for example, were not enticing enough. The winner received £5000 it is true, but the others received sums varying from £100 to £300 and must have been well out-of-pocket. Certainly such rewards would not tempt a canny manufacturer to make expensive tool-room, hand-made, experimental engines—he would probably stick to production

A Pilot and Observer watch an Air Mechanic arming a bomb under an FE2B of No. 149 Squadron, on their aerodrome near St. Omer, 18th July, 1918.

type motor car methods, heavy though they were. Added to this was the strong feeling that the chance of receiving worthwhile orders was poor—certainly the Royal Aircraft Factory was regarded as a malevolent institution taking the bread out of the mouths of the poor aircraft and engine manufacturers. Whatever the truth of these suggestions, there is no doubt that the factory (later the R.A.E.) did invaluable and essential investigation, design, and development work—particularly on aero engines—while the firms in industry did very little.

In due course, when the Factory was under a cloud because of the shortcomings of British aircraft at the Front in 1915, and when great expansion of production was in the offing, the engine manufacturers became interested and eager to make aero engines. It could even be that, as so often before, British industry had been content to allow others to try out new ventures lest there be pitfalls. Many good British inventions and designs have realised their potential only after they have gone abroad.

British manufacturers were not slow however, to make in England under licence, the successful rotary engines the French had been developing—the Gnome, Le Rhone and the Clerget. By 1914 the rotary engines of these manufacturers powered the majority of popular aircraft types. The 50 h.p. 7-cylinder Gnome had grown since 1907 into a whole series of engines of 5, 7 or 9 cylinders in a single row, and 14 and 18 cylinders in two rows. The two row engines were never able to cope with over-heating tendencies in the rear row of cylinders. Le Rhone and Clerget engines were also made in wide variety.

The original 7-cylinder Gnome was very well made, with steel cylinders bored inside and the fins turned outside, from a solid steel billet. The cylinder walls were only one-sixteenth of an inch thick and at the top (where today we would look for the cylinder head), the principal thing to be seen was a large threaded aperture into which the exhaust valve cage was screwed. This cage provided the seat for the valve head and the guide for its stem. The valve was of very light construction and was closed by a small spring and the very considerable centrifugal force created by the revolving engine. The exhaust valve was opened by an over-head rocker and push rod.

The inlet valve was somewhat perilously located in the piston crown, held closed against centrifugal force by counter-weights and a leaf spring. It was, of course, difficult to inspect and exposed to the flame during combustion, but in practice worked very well.

The carburettor was attached to the hollow tailshaft of the engine and the petrol/air mixture drawn into the crankcase. When the exhaust valve closed and the piston descended the reduction of pressure in the cylinder caused the inlet valve in the piston to open automatically (as it did on many motor cycles and cars in the early years of the century, though their automatic inlet valves were mounted in the cylinder head) and the mixture passed into the cylinder. When the induction stroke was complete the piston rose and compressed the mixture as was, and still is, usual in a four-stroke engine.

In 1913/1914 the Gnome appeared in a new guise as the Monosoupape (one valve). The one valve was the exhaust, situated as before on top of the cylinder. This was timed to close after Top Dead Centre on the induction stroke so that a certain amount of cool air was drawn in as the piston started down; the remainder of the induction stroke was completed in the usual way with the exhaust valve closed, causing the usual reduction in pressure over the piston. However, in the Monosoupape design, when the piston reached the bottom of its stroke, ports were uncovered in the cylinder wall, opening into the crankcase. A rich petrol and air mixture rushed in, mixed with the cool air and was compressed by the rising piston as it travelled above the inlet ports at the base of the cylinder, so closing them. This was the substitute for an inlet valve. Following the compression stroke in the usual sequence, the firing stroke was a little unusual in that the exhaust valve opened well before Bottom Dead Centre.

When the piston did reach B.D.C. the pressure had fallen to atmospheric so that little or no mixture passed through the ports into the cylinder. The little that did was beneficial in cooling the piston and exhaust valve as the rising piston pushed out the last remnants of burnt gas on the exhaust stroke.

Like the original 2-valve Gnome, the Monosoupape ran at 1200 r.p.m. but was much more controllable. Instead of the all-on/all-off blip switch, the pilot controlled the exhaust valve timing through a linkage; this allowed the engine to be throttled by regulating the pressure of exhaust gas in the cylinder when the inlet ports opened at B.D.C. The nourishing petrol/air mixture was thus baffled from entering the cylinder to a greater or lesser degree. This allowed a reasonably low slow-running speed and a range of controllable r.p.m. with a maximum quite impossible to achieve on the two-valve Gnome.

The Le Rhone rotaries were notable for their thin cast-iron liners within the steel cylinders, which furnished a much better working surface for the rings, and cast-iron pistons which were used in all of these early engines: also for the ingenious inter-locking slippers on the lower ends of the connecting rods which bore on a drum, instead of the usual articulated rods and pins.

The advantages of the rotary engines were their lightness, smoothness and reliability—they were usually good for 15 hours between overhauls, with reasonably careful handling. There must have been distortion of the thin cylinders but for those days the direction of the cooling medium (air) to the hot spots was more thoroughly effected by the whirling of the engine than the force of water pumps or the art of the pattern maker in providing little passages to reach the

Twin Lewis guns mounted on the top-plane of a Nieuport fighter of No. 111 Squadron in Palestine, 1917–18.

similar hot spots in water-cooled engines. Additionally, the rotary benefited from the fuel cooling within the crankcase and under the pistons. To this was added the liberal drenching with castor oil.

The castor oil was also exhaled in sufficient quantities to drip off the cowling and airframe and affect the pilot's internal economy as efficiently as castor oil taken by the teaspoon.

Ultimately, the rotary engine had to give way to the more civilised in-line, Vee and radial engines because of its crudity, especially of control. It would run really well with little latitude one side or other of a particular r.p.m. and setting of the mixture valve, and the main control was the on-off switch. The more powerful these engines became, the greater the shock to engine mountings and airframes by torque reversals as the blip switch was used. The gyroscopic precession resulting from speeding up the rotating mass of the engine required considerable opposite control to keep the aircraft straight on take off and climb—and sudden loss of power could easily lead to control difficulties. The rotary engines of many of the war aeroplanes were also likely to cause the aeroplane to flick into a spin with little warning. These problems became sufficiently important to open the field to other designs of engine, but these took some time to develop, especially on the Allied side.

While development was under way, the last and best of the rotaries saw service until the end of the War in 1918. This was the Bentley, designed by W. O. Bentley, who was to win lasting fame with his Le Mans winning sports cars. It was first produced as the BR.1 having aluminium cylinders with cast iron liners and, as a real innovation, aluminium pistons. These engines developed 150 h.p. at 1250 r.p.m. and were responsible for making such a formidable aircraft of the Sopwith Camel. The later version was the BR.2 of 230 h.p., which powered the Sopwith Snipe, Salamander and Dolphin.

The near relation of the rotary, the radial, was not widely used before 1918. One of the best examples was the Salmson which was used by the French, particularly in the Caudron bombers. It had no master rod but relied on epicyclic gearing to keep the connecting rods in correct radial position relative to each other.

The air-cooled in-line and Vee engines were among the earliest types on the scene, some being developments of motorcycle and cycle car engines, and engines used for motorcycle pacing of cyclists. Renault in particular, had production facilities to enable him to undertake design and development and make an air-cooled V.8 in 1908. This was developed into the reliable 80 h.p. V.8 which was built under licence in England.

The Royal Aircraft Factory brought out their own series of engines based on the Renault V.8. The R.A.F. version of the V.8. produced 110 h.p. and later they came up with a 12-cylinder version of over 200 h.p. The R.A.F. designs however, were not suitable for fighters, with their large air scoops and unsuitability for close cowling.

As the need for fighters, and bombers too, became recognised, the example of the Germans in engine design clearly became the best to follow. The Mercedes Grand Prix car engines had shown the merits of the in-line 6-cylinder engine with steel cylinders having thin sheet metal water-jackets added, against the older motor car practice of using cast cylinders with cored water passages which could not

German two-seater biplane showing parabellum machine gun.

get the cooling water to the hot spots. The overhead valve gear was usually actuated by a camshaft on top of the cylinders, which were themselves bolted to a light alloy car-type crankcase.

It was a simple layout which broke down easily into main components suitable for large production, easy to modify for greater power or reliability with the minimum upset to production schedules. Most of the German engines were direct drive, possibly as a result of the unfortunate experiences they had with spur-type reduction gears—not the best type of gearing for the purpose.

The Germans, however, were first in the field with super-compressed engines and first with supercharged engines. The super-compressed engines had a compression ratio considerably higher than the fuels and metallurgy of the day could withstand, but the engines were throttled at sea level so that the actual compression ratio realised was the usual ratio of $4\frac{1}{2}$:1 or thereabouts. But at altitude the throttle could be opened wide and full use made of the geometric compression ratio of perhaps 6:1 in the less dense air, to restore sea level power without straining the engine.

In England, Royce had lost his partner Rolls in a flying accident in 1910 and this is said to have prejudiced him against flying in general. The Government wanted him to undertake aero engine manufacture in 1914 and proposed that Rolls Royce should make engines to R.A.F. designs. Rolls did not agree but started design work on an engine of his own, the story being that a Mercedes Grand Prix engine was supplied to him for study. Be that as it may, his first design did show Mercedes design influences, and was the six in-line Hawk of 75 h.p. at 1350 r.p.m.

However, the pressing need of the time was for a 200 h.p. engine so that Hawk design was shelved, and work on the Eagle went forward. This was a V.12 very much like two rows of Hawk cylinders (but of larger capacity) on a common crankcase. It went into production in December 1915 with 320 h.p. which increased to 360 h.p. by early 1918. Its dry weight was about 840 lb and it had an epicyclic reduction gear. The Eagle, like the Hawk, followed the Mercedes practice and had forged steel cylinders with welded-on induction and exhaust ports. There was a single overhead camshaft, two valves and two plugs per cylinder, the latter being fired by four 6-cylinder magnetos.

The Falcon was a scaled-down Eagle which found fame in the Bristol Fighter. It delivered 260 h.p. in mid 1917 and

285 h.p. by the end of the war, for a dry weight of about 675 lb.

Last of the Rolls Royce engines to go into production was the original design, the Hawk, as the motive power for the blimps used for anti-submarine patrols. These were small airships with bare aircraft fuselage slung below and they often stayed in the air on patrol for twenty hours or more. The Hawk proved ideal for this duty and was remarkable for its reliability at a time when few engines had a life of more than 20 hours.

Both German and Allied in-line engines with 6 cylinders and the V.12s suffered crankshaft failures caused by torsional vibration. This was not understood, nor was a cure found until after 1918.

In France, the Spanish Hispano Suiza engine designed by the Swiss (hence the Suiza) Marc Birkigt, broke new ground in the design of the upper half of in-line engines. They were V.8s with the blocks set at 90° to each other and the outstanding feature was that the overhead camshafts and valves were fully enclosed and lubricated; the cams operated direct on to mushroom heads screwed straight on to the valve stems. When it appeared, in 1915, it gave 150 h.p., and later 180 h.p. while geared versions had an output of 220 h.p. at 2200 r.p.m. But the reduction gears gave so much trouble (some French sub-contractors turned out material of a very low standard) that the British Licensee Wolseley decided to develop the direct drive type and finally produced nearly as much power and reliability, but with reduced propeller efficiency.

Armament

The first weapons taken into the air were rifles and pistols. It was nearly impossible for a pilot to fire a rifle with any accuracy and fly an aeroplane at the same time, but observers with rifles had more success. However, some Allied pilots did manage to shoot down German aircraft with revolvers at very close ranges.

The first machine gun to be used in air fighting was the Hotchkiss used in Voisin pusher bombers and in the Morane with steel deflector plates on the propeller blades. The Hotchkiss was very light, little more than a clip-fed rifle, and gave much better service in the air than on the ground, probably because of the cleaner environment in the air. In October 1914 the very first air victory ever recorded went to the observer of a Voisin, who stood up in his cockpit to shoot down an Aviatik. Garros used a Hotchkiss fixed to fire between the armoured propeller blades of his Morane to score the first ever victory with such an arrangement, in April 1915.

The Lewis gun was the standard infantry light machine gun and was also the standard equipment for the observer on the Allied side, with or without (usually the latter) its air-cooling shroud. It was fed from a top-mounted revolving drum holding 47 rounds at first, later 97. It was mounted on a moveable ring around the observer's cockpit which gave a large field of fire. The Lewis was often provided for the pilot, being mounted on the top wing to fire over the propeller disc. It was usually fixed on a mounting which allowed it to be pulled down to the cockpit to change drums—not a favourite occupation because the drums were heavy to manipulate with one hand while flying the aero-

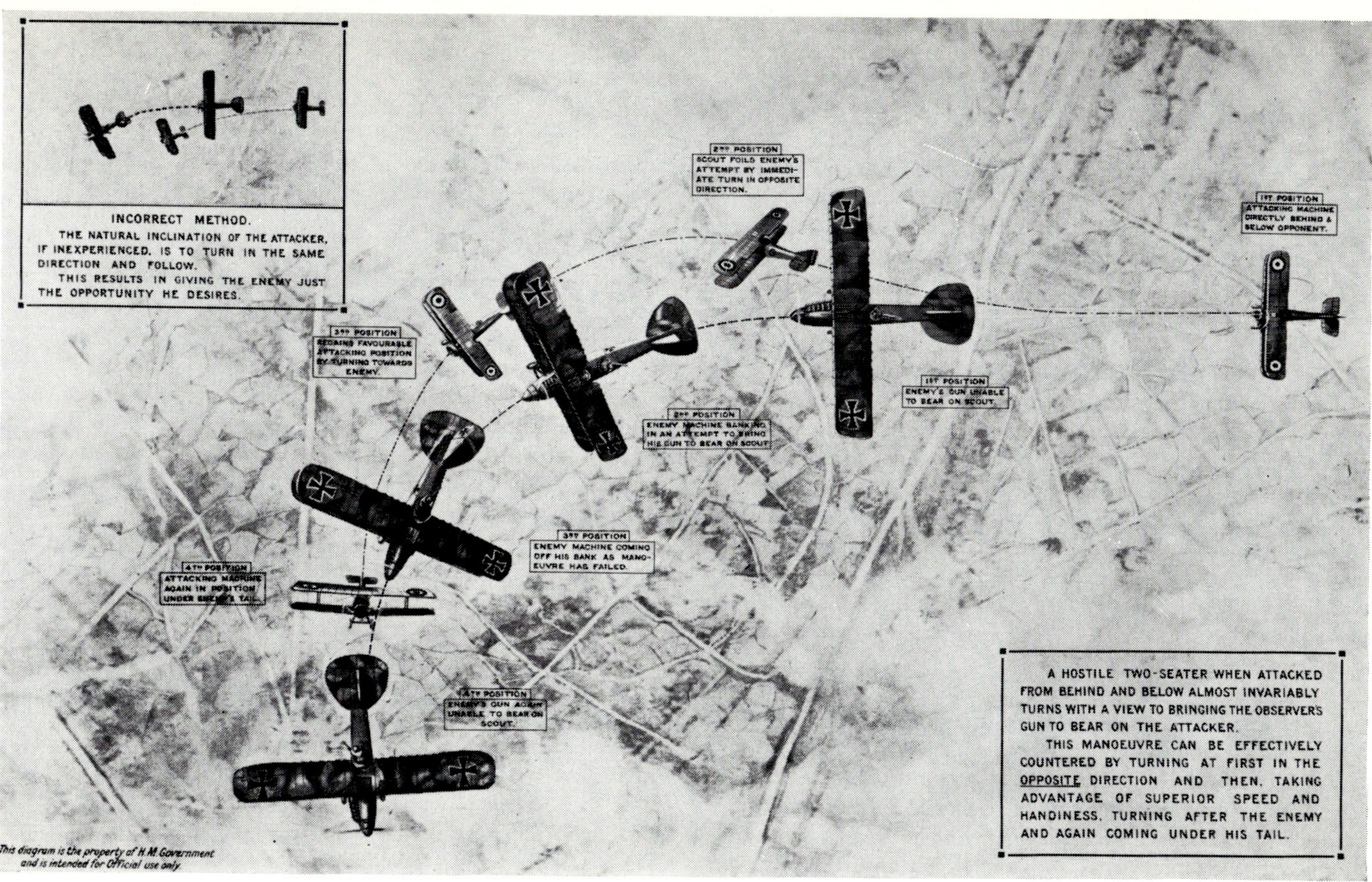

Air Technical Diagram. Dated 21st May, 1918.

plane with the other! This type of mount could also permit firing upward into the belly of an opponent who was passing overhead.

The machine gun usually fitted to Allied fighters firing forward through the propeller by means of a hydraulic or mechanical interrupter timing device, was the Vickers made gun of Maxim design. This was often a double installation, especially in the later stages of the War. At about the same time, the French were successfully using a 37 mm 'cannon' firing through the hollow propeller shaft of the geared Hispano Suiza engine, used principally in the Spad.

Only the Allies called the German machine guns 'Spandaus' after the Berlin Arsenal where the Germans revised the Maxim basic design for aircraft use. They called the light infantry model of these guns—used by the observers—the L.M.G.08 based as it was on the Maxim design of 1908. The heavier model, used in a fixed installation by the pilots, was known as the L.M.G.08/15 because it was derived from the Maxim redesign of 1915. Both guns naturally bore a strong resemblance to the Allies' Lewis and Vickers guns which were also based on Maxim patents.

Some German ground attack aircraft were armed with a 22 mm automatic gun which fired clips of twelve explosive or incendiary shells. Incendiary ammunition was used, particularly for balloon strafing. It was naturally hard on the gun barrels which were quickly corroded by the burning phosphorous. The characteristic of phosphorous (igniting on contact with air) was also employed in 'tracer' ammunition. These had a small amount of phosphorous in a cavity at the base of the bullet which left a smoke trail. Loaded in the proportion of 1 in 5 or 1 in 7 with ordinary or explosive ammunition, it indicated effectively where the stream of bullets was going. The phosphorous had the horrid effect of contaminating wounds and making them difficult to heal.

The usual rate of fire of the guns of both sides was 600 rounds per minute, but by the end of the War this had been increased to 800 or 900.

Very early in the War, boxes of aerial darts or Flechettes were tipped over the side of aëroplanes to rain down on the horses and men of the enemy. They were used rarely and without much success.

The French anticipated the first purpose-built aerial bombs by using artillery shells fitted with tail fins and fused to detonate instantly or with pre-set delay.

The Germans developed a range of tear-drop shaped bombs—at that time the theoretically perfect streamline shape. They had cylindrical tail fins and were in use up to 1916. They had steel noses to aid penetration (the bodies were of cast iron) and were made in 10 lb, 22 lb, 44 lb and 110 lb sizes.

When the German Air Service was organised in 1916 to be independent of the Army, there came into being the German equivalent of the British R.A.E. This body designed a new range of steel bombs of true streamline shape with tail fins imparting a spinning motion—just as with a rifle bullet or artillery shell—which improved stability in flight and accuracy of trajectory. These new bombs were carried horizontally in the bomb trays, unlike the previous design which were stowed vertically. The weights ranged from 27 lb through 110, 220 and 660 lb to 2000 lb.

The R.F.C., as the reconnaissance and artillery spotting

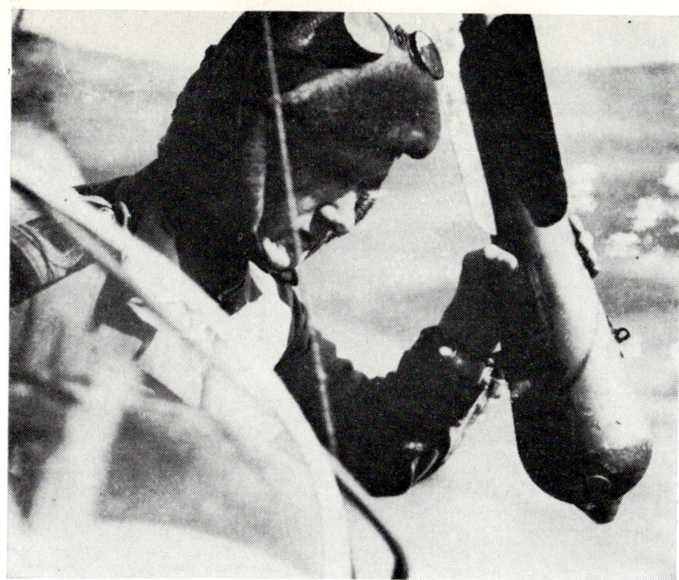

British Pilot photographed dropping a bomb over the side of his aeroplane.

arm of the Army, had no bombers or bombs in the first two years of the war. On the other hand, the R.N.A.S. were keen bombers, having a go at the Zeppelin sheds at Dusseldorf and Cologne in October 1914, and continuing to develop this mode of attack.

By the end of 1915, the R.F.C. had available a series of bombs designed by Woolwich Arsenal and the Royal Aircraft Factory and were beginning to use more and more aircraft in the day-bomber role to drop them. Large numbers of the 112 and 220-pounders were dropped in 1917 and 1918 to support the ground offensives.

By the end of the War, the large bombers of the Independent Air Force could carry the bombs of the S.N. series whose weights ranged from 1600 to 1800 lb. The biggest bomb designed during this period was a 3060 lb giant with which the Handley Page V.1500 would have bombed Berlin had the War lasted into 1919.

Design and Construction

By the time the war began, military aeroplane design was settling down—the tractor biplane was the accepted form. There had been a number of structural failures in the air with monoplanes and this led the authorities to show preference for the biplane. On the Allied side, the pusher biplane remained in vogue for a year or two entirely as a result of the lack of gun interrupter mechanism to allow firing through the propeller.

Practically all the Allied biplanes were built of wood; the fuselages were wire-braced girders with spruce longerons and compression members. Some Allied designers used steel tubing, while in Germany Fokker used little else. Other German constructers used early forerunners of stressed skin construction, carried out with 1 mm and 2 mm ply coverings.

Wood was the most natural choice for aircraft construction in war time, especially when the time came for large-scale production. Apart from its strength and lightness, perhaps the most important reason for its use was that there were many factories which in peace time had been working in wood—making furniture, pianos, builders' joinery and many other commodities. These factories were well equipped with machinery and staffed by skilled and experienced workers. By contrast, the firms producing the lighter kinds of fabricated metal goods were relatively few. Their products were already needed to supply other demands of the war effort. Also, of course, much of the pre-war design experience had been of wooden structures. After 1915 a very great expansion took place and probably more than a million workers were employed on aircraft, engine and equipment production.

From practical knife and fork engineering methods and empirical design before 1914, the R.A.E. in England and their counterparts in France and Germany developed the complicated mathematical bases for the design of aircraft structures. They also set up increasingly effective structural tests and studied the loading of aircraft structures in manoeuvres. At first, tests to destruction were carried out by loading bags of sand on the wings of an aircraft placed upside down; later, bags of shot were used. Little progress was made in understanding aeroelasticity problems during the war years and it was not until the early 1920s that the reasons for structural failures of the wings of some types during 1914/1918 were appreciated.

Wings generally were either of solid spruce spindled out for lightness or of box construction, often utilising plywood. Wings and fuselage were fabric covered (except for the German ply coverings) with metal or ply panels on the forward part of the fuselage.

One item of the specifications of First War aircraft illustrates how design progressed to give higher maximum speeds with inevitably increased landing speeds—the increase in wing loading in successive types, For example, the figures were (lb/sq.ft):—

Various sizes of British bombs with bomb-sights and other equipment.

Sopwith Pup 4.86, Sopwith Camel 6.0, SE.5 7.62.

Mention has already been made of Fokker's predilection for steel tube fuselages, aided by Platz, his master of welding techniques. Also in Germany in 1915, Junkers made the first metal cantilever monoplane, the 'tin donkey' of welded steel including the skin. This did not go into production, but it had successors which saw service. These were the J.2 and the J.4 which was made of Duralumin in 1917.

Duralumin was discovered by accident in Germany by Alfred Wilm in 1909 when he was seeking a means of making strong aluminium cartridge cases. It is an alloy of copper and magnesium with aluminium which can be heat-treated to give the strength of mild steel for a great saving in weight.

RAF Gunnery School at Rang-du-Flers-Verton. A Pilot Officer firing at fixed targets representing German aircraft from a 'cockpit' moving along curving rails. 17th. July, 1918.

Controls and Flying

Wing-Warping. The Wrights used wing-warping instead of ailerons and this means of control was still used in the BE.2 series. In those days, wings were quite flexible unless stiffened by bracing wires in all directions. This flexibility was used to control the aircraft by deliberately warping or twisting the wings by up to a degree of incidence at the wing tips, either plus or minus. This was achieved by connecting some of the bracing wires to the control column, in such a way that moving the stick to the right would twist the right wing to reduce the incidence at the top, while twisting the left wing to increase the incidence at the tip. This would result in a bank and turn to the right.

The drawback to this system was that in gusty weather the forces working on the wing acted through the bracing wires attached to the stick with a violence that the pilot could not easily control. This made flying in gusty weather most uncomfortable, if not hazardous.

Stalling and Spinning. Very large numbers of lives were lost, especially during training in the early part of the War as a result of stalling and spinning. To a great extent these accidents were the result of the stalling speed being only 15 m.p.h. or so below the climbing speed; if the engine failed there was very little time to take corrective action and put the nose down to maintain flying speed. The experienced pilot might do this as a reflex action and live, a novice might stall in a few seconds and die.

The next factor leading to many disasters was psychological—having survived the first onset of a stall, the temptation to turn back to the safety of the aerodrome was immense, but at a height of less than 300 feet it was likely to cause a loss of flying speed, a stall and a crash. However nasty the prospect ahead—trees or houses—there was a better chance of survival by keeping straight on.

After the stall came the spin to earth out of control, from which there was no escape until Major Gooden, the R.A.E. Chief Test Pilot, and Harry Hawker the Sopwith Chief Test Pilot, independently but at more or less the same time, worked out the cure in 1916. Soon after this, the method of preventing a stall by pushing the stick forward, and getting out of a spin by combining this with putting on opposite rudder to the direction of the spin, was well established and spinning became a recognised manoeuvre in air fighting. It could be used to reverse direction to gain an advantage or to retire from a gun fight if the guns jammed, for example.

THE ACES

THE 1914–1918 War justified its name as the Great War in more ways than one. It certainly spread wider geographically than any previous war had done. The number of casualties were many times higher than most other previous wars. It also caused many permanent sociological changes in the world. It involved a far larger proportion of the populations of the combatant nations, whether officially mobilised or not, than had any previous war. Perhaps because of this last feature, more attention was paid to propaganda than ever before.

The two most favoured lines of propaganda were, either to portray the enemy in the worst light possible, including the invention of horrible atrocity stories; or to stimulate recruiting and hearten the populace of one's own side by glorifying the heroes and especially those who fought in the air. Flying was so new that it almost automatically bestowed demi-god status so that little embellishment was needed.

As the War went on, the 'Ace' system developed; based usually on a confirmed score of 5 victories, resulting in the destruction of the enemy aircraft. To secure five confirmed victories might involve shooting down twice that number, as confirmation might not be obtainable for those which came down behind enemy lines. At that time, the accuracy and weight of fire (and the relatively low stressing of the aircraft) were insufficient to cause an aircraft easily to explode or disintegrate in the air.

Generally, it seems that the Germans promoted the 'Ace' system and publicised the Aces themselves more than the Allies did. The British do not seem to have pushed the system so far, while the French were more inclined to build up the prestige of their Escadrilles—Squadron team spirit—before the cult of personality.

The great Aces with scores in excess of 50 confirmed victories came late in the War, when large formations on each side hunted the other and often fought to the death. Earlier on, when air fighting was in the pioneer stage, scores were not so high. That does not detract from the recognition of the high levels of performance by individual pilots on both sides.

One outstanding young German pilot in 1915 was Oswald Boelcke who began his Army service in the Prussian Cadet Corps and then trained as a pilot. When Fokker was demonstrating his new monoplane as it was introduced to squadrons in mid-1915, one of the first pilots he personally instructed was Boelcke.

Not long after, Boelcke was put in charge of a K.E.K. unit and became himself a spearhead of the 'Fokker Menace'. Then soon after converting to the Eindecker himself, he instructed Max Immelmann on the type. Immelmann then took command of another K.E.K. unit and made the 'Fokker Menace' even more terrible for the Allied, and particularly British, slow 2-seaters. He became known as the Eagle of Lille. Both Boelcke and Immelmann were credited with 8 victories each by the beginning of 1916—a great score for those days—and they were both decorated with the highest award, the Blue Max. Immelmann was killed in June 1916 just a year after he had learned to fly an Eindecker.

Boelcke was one of the few Eindecker pilots to survive

until late 1916. During that year he was organising his Jasta, which was the first to become operational, though it was numbered Jasta 2. Boelcke had a great influence on the tactics and organisation of the Jastas and earned the unofficial title of Father of the German Air Service. In October 1916 during a fight with two DH.2s, one wing of his Albatros was damaged by contact with the undercarriage of one of his own flight. Soon afterwards the wing broke up and Boelcke was killed.

Among the pilots recruited by Boelcke was Manfred von Richthofen, a cavalryman who transferred to the air service in 1915. Boelcke trained him and the rest of his asta pilots in team tactics and formation flying and they took up the fight against the British Pushers which had defeated the Eindeckers, in September 1916.

When Jasta 2 received its Albatros fighters late in 1916, von Richthofen made full use of their superior speed and fire power to slaughter the R.F.C.'s slow BE.2cs and BE.12s. The latter was a forlorn hope—a single seater version of the BE.2c. Early in 1917, von Richthofen was decorated and took command of Jasta 2. The aircraft of his Jasta were all painted red and he won fame as the Red Baron, scoring 80 confirmed victories before his death in April 1918.

Werner Voss was another cavalryman who transferred to the air service to get out of the mud, after winning the Iron Cross, First Class, in the trenches. He was a born pilot and a crack shot and he brought down 28 Allied aircraft in the ten months or so after he became a fighter pilot, before taking over a Fokker Triplane in August 1917. Then, in less than a month, he shot down twenty more Allied aircraft bringing his final score to 48 before he was

Oswald Boelcke wearing at his collar the coveted 'Blue Max'.

killed in September 1917. His last fight has been described as one of the epic battles in the air in the first World War. Voss was attacked by five SE.5As led by McCudden (an Ace with a final score of 57) but by using the great manoeuvrability of the Triplane to the full and performing flying feats never before seen, Voss managed to put as many bullets into each of the SE.5As as his own aircraft received. Finally his Triplane dived into the ground from a low altitude, indicating that he must have been badly wounded.

Captain Albert Ball, V.C., D.S.O., M.C., Royal Flying Corps.

The first great British Ace to come to the notice of the public and earn fame by his exploits was Captain Albert Ball, V.C., D.S.O., M.C. He volunteered for the Army at the beginning of the War and later transferred to the R.F.C. flying a BE.2c on artillery spotting. His Squadron had a Nieuport 17 and Ball found in this his ideal aircraft. He had his own fighting method—fly straight at the enemy regardless of the odds and, while passing underneath at close range, pull down the top wing-mounted Lewis and blast the belly out of the enemy aeroplane.

In ten or eleven weeks in 1916 he destroyed ten and forced down another twenty enemy aircraft. Then, after six months spent instructing in England, he returned to France with an SE.5 Squadron and, like Captain Barker, flew SE.5s and his favourite Nieuport but always with a preference for the latter. His score was 44 when he died: his death is a mystery—his SE.5 was seen to dive into cloud and the wreckage of his aircraft found later by the Germans, but there were no wounds to account for his death. Perhaps he just flew into the ground. He was not quite 21 when he died.

Major 'Micky' Mannock, V.C., D.S.O., M.C., was the highest scoring British fighter pilot with a total of at least 73. Transferring from the Royal Engineers to the R.F.C. early in 1917 he flew Nieuport Scouts. By September he had been promoted to Captain, awarded the M.C. and given command of a Flight. Mannock was unusual for his intense hate of the enemy, hunting them down in carefully planned and organised operations. He came back from leave in March 1918 to lead a Flight of SE.5As and increase his score from 23 to 59 in the next three months. After taking command of a Squadron in mid-June the total increased

The cross erected by the Germans over the grave of Captain Albert Ball, shot down by Baron von Richthofen's squadron near Leus on 7th. May, 1917. (*Imperial War Museum*).

to 73 by the end of July when he was brought down by a rifle shot in the petrol tank and killed in the crash.

The most successful Canadian fighter pilot was Lt. Col. W. A. Bishop, V.C., C.B., D.S.O., M.C., D.F.C., who transferred from the Canadian Mounted Rifles to the R.F.C. in 1915 as an Observer. After a crash, he trained as a pilot and joined a Squadron flying Nieuports in 1917 and quickly notched up a succession of victories. He flew many hours a day and in one period of twelve days shot down 25 enemy aircraft. He survived the War, serving in the Royal Canadian Air Force.

Lt. Col. R. Collishaw, C.B., D.S.O., O.B.E., D.S.C., D.F.C. shot down a total of 60 enemy aircraft and was the top scoring R.N.S. pilot of the War. He came from British Columbia, went to sea as a lad and joined the R.N.A.S early in 1916. He was 'B' Flight Commander in the famous 'Naval Ten' Squadron which went to the aid of the R.F.C. on the Western Front. All the pilots of this Flight were Canadians and their Sopwith Triplanes were decorated with various devices and insignia in black paint. Collishaw shot down 3 Albatros in a single fight and a total of 16 in 27 days. He was twice shot down himself but escaped injury and survived the War, serving in the R.A.F. and reached the rank of Air Vice-Marshal.

Major James McCudden, V.C., D.S.O., M.C., M.M. joined the R.F.C. from the Royal Engineers in 1913 and went to France as an air mechanic in 1914. He flew officially as an observer while gaining experience unofficially as a pilot on a single seater Morane, before going back to England for flying training. In mid-1916 he was posted as a Flight Sergeant to a DH.2 fighter squadron. He was commissioned at the beginning of 1917 and spent six months training new pilots. In August 1917, when his score was seven, he took command of a Flight of SE.5s and in the next six months raised his score to 57 or more—on at least two occasions shooting down four in a day. After a period of instructing in England, he returned to France to take command of a squadron, but was killed in a crash when his engine failed after take-off.

Many of the older generation of Aces had a motor racing background; Captain E. Rickenbacker of the U.S. Air Service was an example. In fact, he was in England in 1917 on motor racing business and at the height of his fame as a racing driver when he became interesting in flying. This coincided with America's entry to the War. Returning to America he joined the Army and went to France as driver for General Pershing (U.S. Army C-in-C).

By March 1918 he had transferred to the Air Service as an Engineer Officer, learned to fly in his spare time, and been posted to an operational squadron—the U.S. 94th. Rickenbacker flew the first American patrol over the German lines on March 19th. He built up his score to eleven by the end of September, when he took command of the 94th and by the end of the War he was credited with 26 confirmed victories. After the War he returned to car racing, became Vice-President of American Airways in 1932, then General Manager of Eastern Airlines in 1938 and then bought Eastern Airlines himself. He died in 1973 at the age of 83.

Captain René Fonck was the top-scoring Allied Ace with 75 confirmed victories—5 less than Richthofen. Quite possibly his actual score was half as great again, but many of his victims crashed behind the German lines and could not be confirmed. He managed a transfer from the Army to the Aviation Service in early 1915 and joined a Caudron Squadron in June. He scored an unusual success when he captured a German aircraft and crew by flying so close beside and above it that he contrived to bully it into landing behind the French lines.

Soon after this he converted to fighters and was posted

Captain Baron Manfred von Richthofen's pursuit flight on the Western Front. The Red Baron and his men, left to right: Sabastian Festner, Unidentified officer, Rittmeister Baron von Richthofen, Oberleutnant Baron Lothar von Richthofen, Oberleutnant Kurt Wolff.

in March 1917 to the famous Cigognes (Stork) Escadrille 103, flying S.P.A.D.s. Several times he shot down doubles and twice in 1918 he shot down six aircraft in one day. He was a remarkable shot and often used only 5 or 6 rounds to achieve a kill. He died in 1953.

Captain Georges Guynemer was the second highest

Major Chevalier Willy Coppens de Houthulst, D.S.O., M.C. Ace balloon buster of World War I.

scoring French Ace, with 54 confirmed victories. But he was probably the favourite in the hearts of the French. Although 20 when he finally graduated from flying training, he looked so frail and youthful that tough French Army officers were quite upset to see him—it appeared that they were calling on the last reserves of children to fight the Boche! In fact, he had failed two medicals in 1914 before being accepted.

Guynemer joined the Stork Group, which consisted of four Escadrilles—Nos. 3, 26, 73 and 103. His was then called MS.3 because it was flying Morane Saulnier monoplanes. Later it was called N.3, in the French manner, when re-equipped with Nieuport Scouts, and finally S.P.A. 3 when it received S.P.A.D.s.

He was shot down seven times, on one occasion being rescued by a timely charge of the French infantry when he crashed between the lines. His health deteriorated but he insisted on continuing to fly until, when not quite 23, he disappeared on a flight in September 1917, never to be found. His final score was 54.

Lt. Charles Nungesser was rated No. 3 of the French Aces with 45 victories. Another with a car racing background, he had taught himself to fly in South America before the War. In 1914 he joined a Hussar regiment, transferred to the air service in 1915 and was shot down in a Voisin on reconnaissance. Late in 1915 he joined Escadrille N.65 (Nieuports) and started to score heavily and also, unfortunately, to crash heavily, so that he had many visits to hospital to re-set broken bones. He often had to be carried to his aeroplane and lifted into the seat. However, he survived the War only to be lost on a Trans-Atlantic flight in 1927; the aircraft in which he was lost was painted with the same grim, black devices as his war time Nieuport —a heart, skull and crossbones, two candles and a coffin.

The small Belgian Air Force tended to be the poor relation and to get the aircraft the bigger boys did not want. However, the big boys certainly did the Belgians a good turn when they gave them the Hanriot HD.1.

It was with this type that Willy Coppens finally made his name with a top Belgian score of 37 including 26 balloons, making him second highest scoring balloon buster of the War.

At the beginning of the War he was in the Army but he transferred to the air service late in 1915, being posted to a 2-seater squadron in mid-1916. In July 1917 he went to a fighter squadron and soon after began his career on the HD.1, at first without success. Soon he acquired the technique and scored regularly. He was knighted for his exploits and took the title of de Houthulst, after the forest over which he scored many of his victories.

ALLIED AIR SERVICES

LEFT: Lieutenant, French Aviation Services. This officer wears the dark blue-black of the French 'GENIE' or Engineers, under whose direction the French Flying Corps was formed. Officers transferred to Aviation usually continued to wear the uniforms of the original unit: Cavalry, Infantry, Foreign Legion, etc. Uniforms were worn with aviation insignia on caps and collars, and pilots' wings, squadron insignia, etc., on the tunic. The usual wide range of official and unofficial flying gear was also worn. RIGHT: Belgian Pilot Officer 1918. La Force Aerienne Belge was formed in 1911 at Brasschaet, Antwerp. After Belgium was overrun by the Germans her Army, including the small air force, was re-organised, and uniformed by Great Britain. Khaki was the colour adopted by all Arms. This officer wears his pilots' wings, a thick sweater under his tunic, and riding boots. He is lucky to have a fine Bearskin overcoat—a real blessing on a cold dawn patrol.

GREAT BRITAIN

LEFT: Officer, Royal Flying Corps. He wears the R.F.C.'s distinctive double breasted jacket, worn by all ranks. Officers who transferred from other units usually clung to their original uniforms, or wore them out flying. A variety of breeches were worn, with high black or brown boots, or puttees and ankle boots. Officers customarily carried walking sticks. He wears his pilots' wings on his breast and his rank badges on his shoulder straps. His R.F.C. cap and collar badges are bronze. RIGHT: Officer, R.F.C. in flying dress, 1915. This soft-leather flying coat was usually worn, over Regimentals and any number of other garments depending on weather, season and fancy! Every kind of unorthodox dress saw service (including pyjamas and slippers!). This officer wears sweater and slacks, and a pair of comfortable civilian shoes. In colder weather, boots, overtrousers, scarves, etc., were worn. Later in the war one-piece flying suits were introduced, some electrically heated.

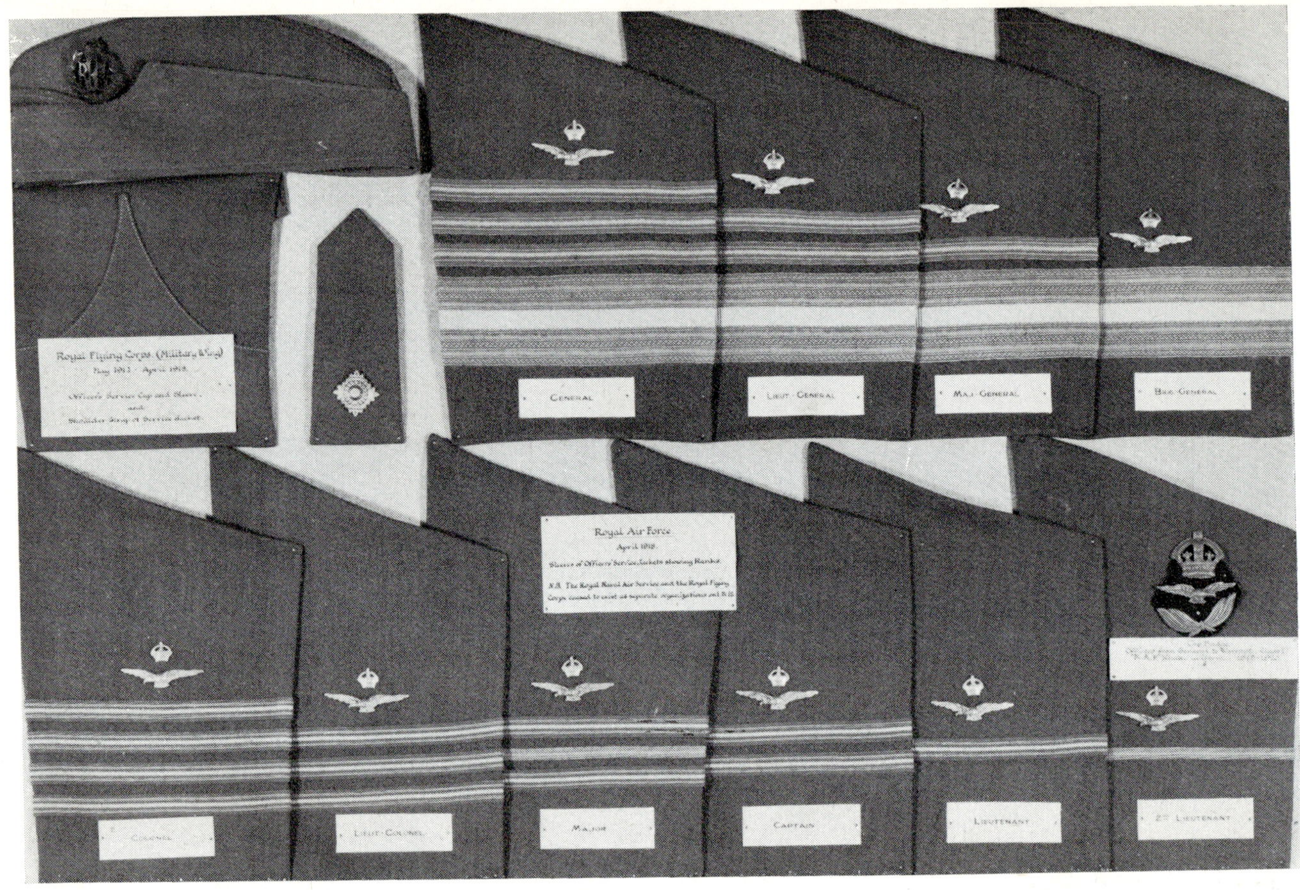
Royal Flying Corps (Military Wing)
General
Lieut-General
Maj-General
Brig-General
Royal Air Force
April 1918
Colonel
Lieut-Colonel
Major
Captain
Lieutenant
2nd Lieutenant

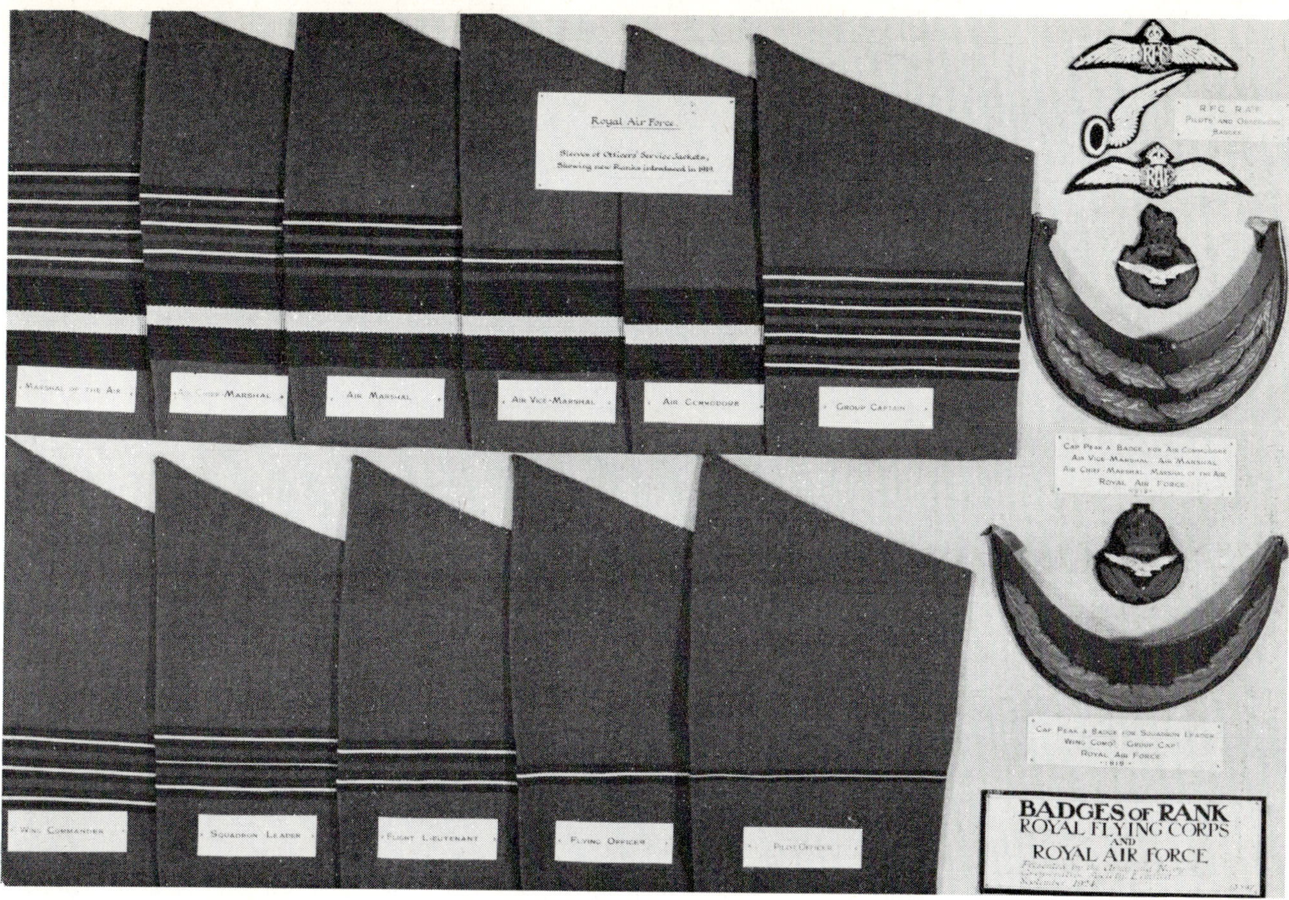
Royal Air Force
Marshal of the Air
Air Marshal
Air Vice-Marshal
Air Commodore
Group Captain
Wing Commander
Squadron Leader
Flight Lieutenant
Flying Officer
Pilot Officer
BADGES OF RANK
ROYAL FLYING CORPS
AND
ROYAL AIR FORCE

GERMAN AIR SERVICE

Lieutnant, Feld Flieger Abteilung, 1914–15. As with the Allies, officers transferred to the German Air Corps wore the uniforms of their original units, adopting suitable flying kit when necessary, and wearing the Air Corps winged-propeller insignia on the shoulder straps and a small metal pilot's badge low on the left breast of their tunic. This officer wears a padded leather helmet and black leather jacket over his Hussar Field Service uniform. A Feld Flieger Abteilung was a Field Flying Section, usually of 6 Aeroplanes. RIGHT: Officer, Feld Flieger Bataillone No. 2 1914–15.

This officer wears the red and black trimmed uniform of the German Air Service proper, with puttees and breeches. He wears his pilots badge and iron cross on his tunic and at his collar the 'Pour le Merite'—Germany's highest award for bravery—the coveted 'Blue Max'. The two small round badges on his Field service cap were worn by all German troops—the top one is the black, white and red colours of Germany, the lower the black and white of Prussia. Other states within Germany had their own colours.

LEFT: Senior officer of Flieger Abteilung 1915–18. This figure illustrates the change to German Army Field uniforms authorised in 1915 when the troops of all armies were ordered to adopt a plain unpiped jacket (Bluse) with a fly-front. Leather belts were ordered to be blackened. In fact, German troops were still not fully equipped with new uniforms when the war ended. RIGHT: Observer, Cold weather flying kit, 1918. This officer wears all the spare clothes he can under his leather flying coat, leather trousers and sheepskin overboots, and several pairs of gloves. Over his clothes is buckled the harness for his 'Heinecke' parachute—which saved many lives during the last months of the war. Around his neck hang binoculars and a fur muff, into which he could thrust his cold hands between observations. All kinds of warm clothing were adopted by the flyers of all nations, often captured items were used. Warm one-piece suits were issued during the latter part of the war and captured British 'Sidcot' flying suits were used by some German airmen.

LEFT: Hauptman Ritter von Schleich, commanding officer of No. 4 fighter squadron (Jagdstaffel) standing beside his black 'Albatros'. He wears a leather flying coat and helmet, puttees and boots. At his neck the 'Blue Max'. RIGHT: Lieutenant Max von Mulzer, killed in 1916. Von Mulzer wears the uniform of his original Uhlan (Lancer) Regiment, with his pilots badge low on his left breast. Richthofen too wore Uhlan uniform and this has led more than one film maker to dress all his German flyers as Uhlans. The Cavalry attracted young officers who liked to 'cut a dash'. They jumped at the chance to become the 'Cavalry of the Air' and to carry on a more chivalrous war in the skies above the squalor of the trenches.

AIRCRAFT PORTRAIT GALLERY

Fighter and Reconnaisance Aircraft over the Western Front

SE5A Scouts of 85 Squadron, at St. Omer Aerodrome, 21st. June 1918.

AIRCRAFT COLOUR SCHEMES

Spad XIII CI of the 22nd Aero Squadron American Army 1918.

Albatros D.V. Josta 27, flown by Lt. Herman Göring (May 1917).

S.E.5a flown by Major J. T. B. McCudden (57 confirmed victories).

Typical German lozenge pattern fabric.

Spad XIII 94th Aero Squadron,
American Expeditionary Force
flown by Capt. Eddie Rickenbacker

Nieuport 17c-1 flown by Sgt. R. Soubiran
of the "Escadrille" Lafayette, Western front 1916

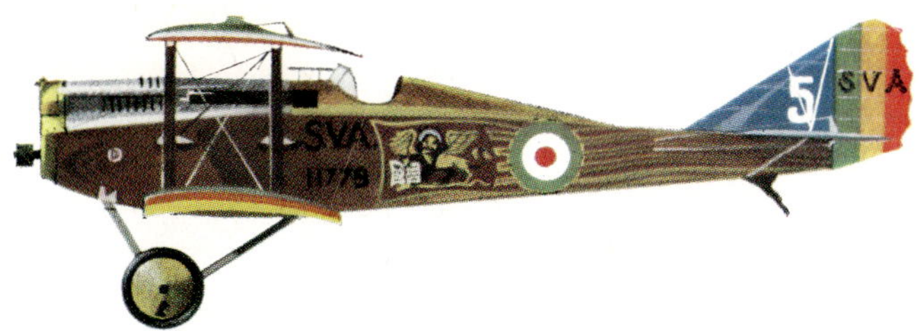

S.V.A.5 of the 87° Squadriglia
Ricognizione " La Serenissima ",
Aeronautica Militare

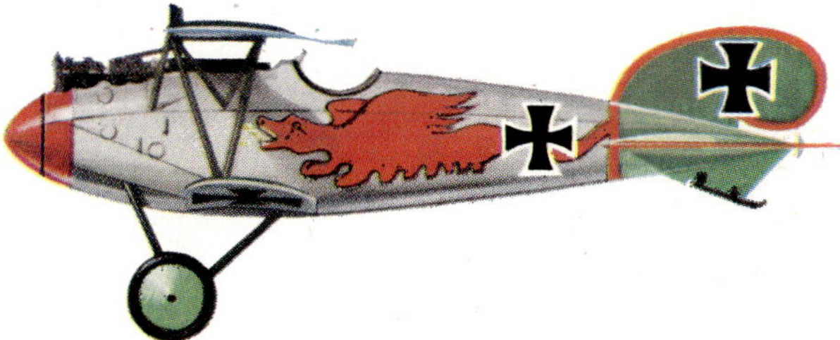

Albatros DV, Jasta 5,
flown by Lt. Hans Joachim
Von Hipple.

Two R.F.C. Officers scan the skies above the aerodrome at Rang du Fliers 1918. The officer at left wears full R.F.C. uniform, the other wears army tunic with flying helmet and pilots' wings on his left breast. His military rank is on his cuffs. The telescope mounting has been improvised from the front wheel of a bicycle.

ABOVE: Women played an important role in war for the first time during 1914–18. This won them some much deserved equality of status with men, and the vote. Many served near the front line as drivers, nurses, etc. Here is a rather pretty woman driver of the R.F.C. RIGHT: Air Mechanic, R.F.C. in full marching order. Other ranks uniforms were of a slightly lighter khaki than those of the officers, and their cap buttons and badges were brass instead of bronze. Note his revolver, with attached lanyard worn around the neck.

NATIONAL MARKINGS ON AIRCRAFT 1914-1918

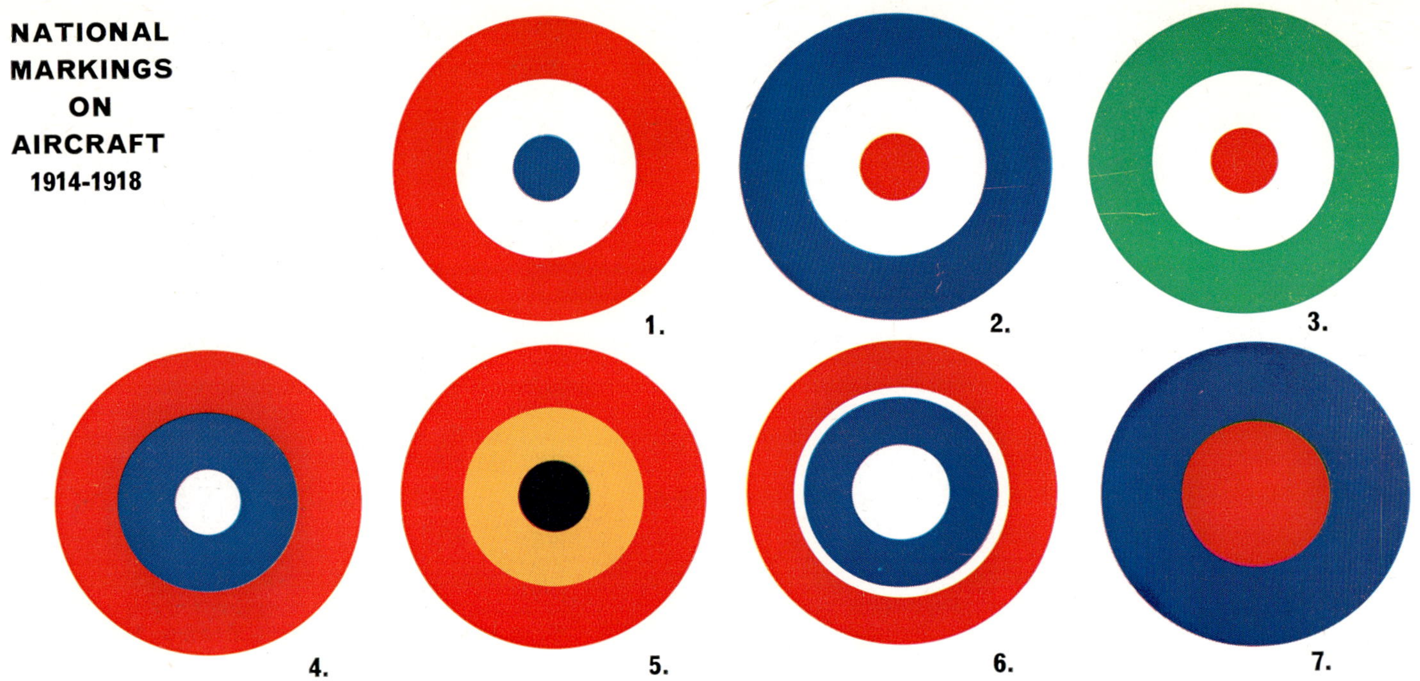

1. France 1914–18 (wings only). 2. Great Britain. 3. Italy 1915–18. 4. American Expeditionary Force 1917–18. 5. Belgium 1915–18. 6. Imperial Russia 1915–17. 7. Great Britain Night Flying Aircraft from August 1918.

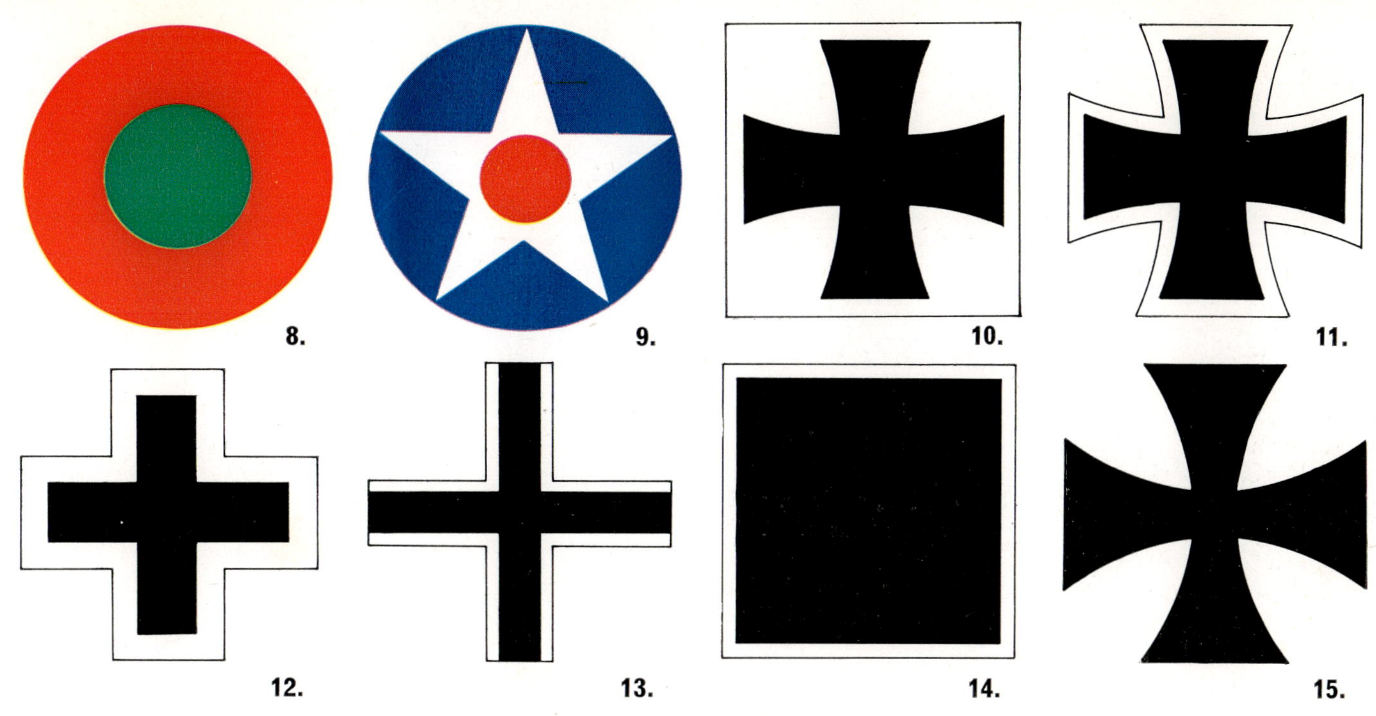

8. Portugal 1916–18. 9. U.S. Navy from May 1917. 10. Germany 1914–15. 11. Germany 1915–17. 12. Germany 1917–18. 13 .Germany 1918. 14. Turkey 1915–18. 15. Bulgaria 1914–18. Note, Austria-Hungary same as Germany.

BE. 2a, b, c

IN 1911 the Army Aircraft Factory had no authority to design or build an aeroplane as they would very much like to have done. So, encouraged by the success of a similar gambit previously, they took the opportunity when asked to repair an aeroplane, to ask for the official order to cover 'reconstruction'.

Thus it was that the aeroplane which the Duke of Westminster had presented to the War office went into the Factory as a damaged Voisin and emerged so entirely 'reconstructed' that it was, in fact, a new aeroplane designed by Geoffrey de Havilland and F. N. Green. It was called BE.1 which then stood for 'Bleriot Experimental' (Bleriot was credited with being the originator of the tractor aeroplane). Later BE came to be translated as 'British Experimental'.

The BE.1 owed its Wolseley 60 h.p. engine, radiator and petrol tank to the Voisin; everything else was new. It made its first flight early in 1912.

Just a year later, BE.1 was joined by a very similar brother called BE.2, which had a 70 h.p. Renault engine. During August 1912, Geoffrey de Havilland, with a passenger, set up a new British altitude record, using BE.2 and reaching 10,560 ft in 45 minutes.

Orders were placed for a slightly modified version, the BE.2a which appeared just a year later. The Factory made very few the main contractors being British and Colonial Aircraft Co. (later British Aeroplane Co.) and Vickers.

Early in 1914, cockpit protection was improved and control system modifications were made, though wing warping on the Wright model was still used rather than ailerons. The engine installation was unchanged. This version was the BE.2b.

R.F.C. Squadrons Nos. 2 and 4 flew to France with their BE.2as and 2bs on 13th. August, 1914, and one of their BE.2as was the first British aircraft to land in France after war broke out.

The first award of a V.C. to the British air services went to Lt. Rhodes-Moorhouse of No. 2 Squadron, who was fatally wounded while dropping a single 100 lb bomb on an important railway junction.

The next development was to fit the R.A.F. engine and a V type undercarriage and this version was called the BE.2c. All the variants remained together in squadron service until well into 1915 and did good work as reconnaissance and observation aircraft. They were much used for artillery spotting; operating at 3000 to 4000 ft they signalled to the British batteries by Aldis lamp.

Armament was limited to pistols, carbines and rifles carried by pilots and observers; grenades and light hand-delivered bombs or a single 100 lb bomb were occasionally carried.

Performance—BE.2a Max speed at 7000 ft: 65 m.p.h. Climb to 7000 ft: 35 min. Service ceiling 10,000 ft.

W.A.—4

FE.2B

The pusher aeroplane seemed to the British in 1914 to be the only answer to the problem of carrying a forward firing gun. The idea of firing through the propeller appears to have occurred to no one until the Germans made deadly use of their interrupter gear.

The FE.2 was designed just before de Havilland left the Royal Aircraft Factory, but he probably had little to do with it, though he obviously had the pusher solution in mind when designing his own DH.1 and DH.2. The next R.A.F. version was the FE.2a with a 100 h.p. Green engine. This was later replaced by the 120 h.p. Austro Daimler engine built by Beardmore. Twelve FE.2as were built and were delivered to the R.F.C. in France.

More power was provided in the FE.2b by a 160 h.p. Beardmore engine and these were successful in mid-1916 against the Fokker monoplanes with their synchronised gun. The death of German Ace, Max Immelmann (the inventor of the Immelmann turn—a roll off a loop) was credited to an FE.2b. After attacking one, Immelmann's Fokker monoplane dived away and broke up in the air. The Germans said it broke up because of previous damage caused by anti-aircraft fire. Another theory is that the interrupter gear failed and he shot off his own propeller and the vibration broke up the aircraft.

Because of the necessary extra booms, struts and wire, the pusher was inevitably slower than a tractor of comparable power. There was also the danger of an engine blow-up damaging the structure; in a crash the engine was likely to move forward and crush the pilot.

Morane Saulnier Type N

This neat little monoplane displayed in every feature that it was of decidedly pre-war design, following the Type L, which was called a 'Parasol' because the wing was raised above the fuselage, over the pilots head. It might not have become famous but for the fact that it was one of the earliest single seater scouts to carry a machine gun which could be fired through the propeller, and so lay claim to the appellation of 'fighter'. In fact, the Type L Morane Saulnier was the first to have this great advantage.

Morane Saulnier—Raymond Saulnier and Robert Morane—were attempting in 1913 with the collaboration of the Hotchkiss machine gun works to develop a synchronising mechanism. They did not succeed by the time war started and the French War Office took back the borrowed gun. The reason for their failure lay not in the mechanism but in the ammunition; this did not have a consistent rate of burning, so that slow-fire or hang-fire cartridges caused the bullets to lag and hit the propeller. Before finally giving up they tried the somewhat desperate expedient of allowing the bullets to hit the propeller but provided steel deflector plates to save the blades from damage. This met with some success but was dropped when the gun was taken away.

However, two pilots of Escadrille 23 each well known for their flying feats before the War, were also looking for an answer to the problem. They were Eugene Gilbert and Roland Garros. They heard of the unfinished experiments and obtained the permission of G.H.Q. to borrow a gun and visit the Morane Saulnier Works. There an aircraft was supplied, the gun and steel deflector plates fitted, and Garros carried out the first ever flying firing trials, early in 1915.

When these were successfully finished Garros returned to the Front and at the beginning of April 1915 shot down an Albatros two-seater. He followed this up, to the consternation of the Germans, by shooting down four more—all in less than three weeks. Unfortunately, before April was out, Garros made a forced landing behind the German lines after being hit by ground fire, and the secret was out.

The Germans ordered Fokker to make a similar device and fit it to his monoplanes. Fokker went one better; in a week his staff came up with the design of a synchronising gear and this was fitted to the E.1 and later marks.

Contrary to widely held belief, Garros was in fact flying a Type L Parasol when he was shot down, and not a Type N.

Nieuport 12

The success of the Bleriot Monoplane led to most small, single and two-seaters built before 1914 being monoplanes. Perhaps the first signpost to a different line came with the Sopwith Tabloid seaplane which came home ahead of the heavier French monoplanes in the 1914 Schneider Trophy Race. The Tabloid had a top speed of 100 m.p.h. and landed at 40 m.p.h. Its lightness and speed was due largely to the ease of stressing and inherent strength of the biplane—built on the lines of that well-known structure, the bridge.

Because of the difficulty of bracing monoplanes by external wires to drag-producing king posts above the cockpit and queen posts below, and the lack of knowledge of stressing such constructions, these monoplanes were either heavy or weak, sometimes both. There were so many structural failures in the air that the monoplane design for fighters was banned for new British designs after 1914.

The Nieuport designer produced a series of aeroplanes which tried—and largely succeeded—to have the best of both worlds. His scaled down biplanes were nearly all sesquiplanes; that is to say, the lower wing was small in span and chord and was present essentially to provide the bridge-type bracing structure, most of the lift being provided by the top wing. This arrangement also allowed a good view downwards—important for a fighter pilot.

The Nieuport 12 was a two-seater fighter which came into service with the French early in 1915. Its smaller single-seater brother was the Type 11, affectionately known as 'Bébé'.

Both Type 11 and Type 12 were armed with a machine gun on the top wing, firing above the propeller disc. The type 12 also having another gun on a moveable mounting in the rear cockpit.

DH.2

Geoffrey de Havilland was designing his own aeroplanes some years before the war. His second was a single seater pusher type which he built in 1910, powered by a 45 h.p. engine which he also designed. He learned to fly it in September 1910 and in December joined the Army Balloon Factory as test pilot and assistant designer. The War Office bought his aeroplane for £440 and called it FE.1—Farman (i.e. pusher) Experimental No. 1.

Following the lines of the FE.1, the FE.2 was designed with a nacelle for the pilot, with a Maxim gun mounted in it. This first FE.2 was replaced by a redesign on similar lines, again called FE.2, but this one was lost in a crash.

Soon after this, in June 1914, de Havilland moved to the Aircraft Manufacturing Co. and his first design to be made there was the DH.1. This appeared in early 1915 almost simultaneously with the FE.2a, the Royal Aircraft Factory's latest redesign of the FE.2.

Possibly because of the lack of a British gun synchronising mechanism to allow firing through the propeller (though one had been patented in England, and others in different countries before 1914) de Havilland's next design was again a pusher, with a gun on a moveable mounting in the nose. It was powered by a 100 h.p. Gnome Monosoupape ('single valve') engine. The prototype went to France in mid-1915 for evaluation. Within a few days it came down behind the German lines and turned over; the pilot died. It is not certain whether it was shot down and the pilot fatally wounded or whether its unreliable engine failed and the pilot died of his injuries after the crash.

Production aircraft were delivered to squadrons late in 1915 and at last British pilots had an aircraft which could attack the German monoplane fighters. However, they were hampered by the 'wobbly gun mounting' which the authorities would not allow the Squadrons to modify, by the lack of speed especially in a dive, and by the unreliability of the Monosoupape engine which could shed cylinders and other components to the detriment of the pusher's tail booms. In spite of this, the DH.2 gave remarkable service, helping to defeat the 'Fokker Menace' and preserve British air supremacy over the Somme offensive.

Performance—Max speed at 10,000 ft: 77 m.p.h. Climb to 10,000 ft: 25 min.

38

Fokker Monoplanes

Anthony Fokker was a brilliant pilot who had many ideas, not all of them good. He relied largely on his designers in the first instance, and often produced an excellent aeroplane after modifying it to suit his high standards of controllability and handling in the air. After four unsuccessful designs, which he was unable to get right by test flying and alterations, he dismissed the designer. Besides appointing the assistant to become Chief Designer, he decided to copy the Morane Saulnier H. monoplane he had seen performing so successfully. He bought a crashed example cheaply for study. Only the principal shapes and relationships were copied, the wooden fuselage of the Morane Saulnier were replaced by a stronger steel tube structure in the design of which Reinhold Platz (a welding specialist, later to become Fokker's Chief Designer) had a hand. The Fokker wings were stronger and of different section.

The resulting aeroplane was known as the M.5 and was fitted with an 80 h.p. Oberursel engine (a Licence-built French Gnome rotary). A small number of M.5s saw service in the early days of the war, but were soon withdrawn from operational service due to losses caused by the unreliability of the engine. They continued to be used for fast communications and training as they had the rather unusual provision of a bench seat which allowed a passenger to squeeze in behind the pilot.

Fokker received orders for a single-seater monoplane fighter; this was the E.I and was an instant success due, in large part, to it having a synchronised machine gun firing through the propeller. It was highly effective against slow, almost defenceless Allied reconnaissance aircraft.

The E.I closely followed the design of the M.5, retaining the bench seat; it also had a hole cut in the floor for downward view, closed by a lever-operated flap. However, due to being rushed into production with little development flying, a number of faults appeared. Minor redesign to eliminate these faults and install the 100 h.p. Oberursel engine gave rise to the E.II. One alteration was to reduce the wing area to gain more speed. It was more difficult to fly, but no faster.

The next version was the E.III which had the wing span increased by nearly 2 ft to gain more speed, this time with more success. The first E.III appeared at the Front in August 1915 and for a time all three variants were in use at once. Probably about 450 were built altogether.

Armament—E.I, E.II: one LMG.08 machine gun. E.III: usually as E.I, E.II, but sometimes with two LMG.08s.

Performance—Max. speed: E.I, E.II, 81 m.p.h.; E.III, 87 m.p.h. Climb to 3,000 ft: E.I, E.II, 7 min; E.III, 5 min.

Fok. E III 210

Sopwith 1½ Strutter

The unusual name of one-and-a-half strutter orginated from the unusual arrangement of struts at the inner ends of the top mainplanes (there was no centre section) which joined at the point of an inverted V strut over the fuselage. Outwardly inclined struts from the top longerons to support the top wings completed a W strut formation. The story was coined that it was to have been a two bay (two strutter) biplane but finished up as a 1½ strutter.

The Admiralty originally ordered a batch of 50 two-seater 1½ strutters fitted with Clerget 110 h.p. engines and the first was delivered early in 1916. Fortunately, it could have a synchronised gun firing through the propeller, as the 'Fokker Scourge' and adverse publicity had at last awakened the British authorities to the need for it. The 1½ strutter was one of the first British aircraft so fitted. It was also the first tractor two-seater fighter which gave practical armament to both pilot and observer and established the formula later to be confirmed by the Bristol Fighter.

The first aircraft went into service in April 1916. The Admiralty had long wanted to make long distance raids into Germany. Although small, the 1½ Strutter was capable of long range, so a single-seat version was made by covering the rear cockpit and stowing 4 × 65 lb bombs horizontally and internally, to be dropped through bomb doors opening under the weight of the bombs. Besides modifying some two-seaters in this way, a batch of single-seater bombers was ordered.

The R.N.A.S. planned to have a bomber Wing in the Spring of 1916, to include about 70 1½ Strutters, half single-seat bombers and half as two-seater escort fighters. This was probably the first strategic bombing force ever formed.

However, the plans for air support of the Somme offensive in Spring 1916 showed the R.F.C. required an additional 12 squadrons for day bombing and ground support. They were not available and the Admiralty were asked for help. The R.N.A.S. bomber Wing operations were delayed until July 1916 as more than sixty 1½ Strutters were handed over to the R.F.C.

Many more were built both for the Admiralty and the War Office and the French built several thousand for their own Air Service, making a total of about 6000 altogether.

Performance—Max. speed at 10,000 ft: 97 m.p.h. Climb to 10,000 ft: 20 min.

Sopwith Pup

The Pup was a single-seater fighter which followed the 1½ Strutter off the drawing boards of Herbert Smith and his Sopwith design staff. Its ancestry was obvious and, as it was noticeably smaller than the 1½ Strutter, the flying services nick-named it the Pup. This infuriated officialdom and stern orders were promulgated that the aircraft was always to be referred to by its official description and type number, so the flying services *always* called it the Pup.

Its construction, like the 1½ Strutter before it, was conventional. The structure was of spruce, fabric covered except for the decking around the cockpit which was ply-covered and some had transparent covering of the centre section to improve upward view.

The first Pups went to the R.N.A.S. early in 1916 powered by the 80 h.p. Clerget and were an instant success. Its performance on 80 h.p. was outstanding and its handling was perfect. More were ordered for the R.N.A.S. and nearly all had the 80 h.p. le Rhone engine.

At the end of 1916 deliveries began to the R.F.C. Prior to this, the R.N.A.S. formed a special Squadron No. 8 to help the R.F.C. on the Somme. It became known as 'Naval Eight' and in the last two months of 1917 shot down 20 enemy aircraft with their Pups. It came into wide use with the R.F.C. in 1917 and though outclassed in speed by the October of that year, remained in service till December by virtue of its really excellent manoeuvreability at altitude. Withdrawn at the end of 1917 it was used for training and was very popular. Nearly 2000 were made in all.

The association with the Navy through the R.N.A.S. led to trials being carried out with deck landings, flying off 20 foot platforms on cruisers and ditching with inflatable flotation bags. The first deck landings were actually made in August 1917 and this and other developments in association with the Navy led to many modifications being made.

Armament—R.N.A.S. and R.F.C. had one synchronised Vickers machine gun. R.F.C. Pups could carry a load of small bombs. R.N.A.S. could have eight le Prieur rockets for attacking balloons or Zeppelins. Shipboard Pups had a Lewis gun on a tripod in front of the cockpit, firing upwards.

Performance—Max. speed at 10,000 ft: 105 m.p.h. Climb to 10,000 ft: 14 min.

DH.4

The DH.4 was designed by Geoffrey de Havilland around the 160 h.p. Beardmore engine for reconnaissance and bombing but the first prototype flew in 1916 with the new B.H.P. (Beardmore-Halford-Pullinger) engine of 200 h.p. The second prototype had the Rolls Royce 250 h.p. engine (later known as the Eagle III and IV).

The first 50 production aircraft came out early in 1917 and had the entire forward fuselage covered with plywood, needing no bracing wires. The pilot sat under the centre section which had a transparent window to assist upward view.

Unfortunately, the supply of Rolls Royce engines failed and to power the 690 additional aircraft ordered, the decision was taken to use the B.H.P. engine. The B.H.P. was re-designed for maximum production and renamed the Siddeley Puma. Engine production delays were lengthy and by the time it was in good supply in 1918, it was obsolete. Some DH.4s had the Factory's R.A.F.3a water cooled V-12 engine, designed in 1914. It did not earn a good name in service. The best DH.4 version was that fitted with the R.R. Eagle VIII of 375 h.p. About 2100 in total were produced in 1917/1918.

Armament: One synchronised Vickers machine gun firing forward, one Lewis gun on Scarff mounting in rear cockpit. 4 × 112 lb bombs could be carried.

Performance—Max. speed m.p.h.: climb to 10,000 ft: Siddeley Puma 116 at 10,000 ft: 25 min. R.R. Eagle III 113 at 10,000 ft: 17 min. R.R. Eagle VIII 133 at 10,000 ft: 9 min.

DH.9

The War Office decided in mid 1917 to increase the total number of R.F.C. Squadrons to 200; most of the new squadrons would be equipped with day bombers.

A new type of aircraft would be needed but as the DH.4 fighter-reconnaissance type was already planned and soon to come into production, modified DH.4s would be used initially in the day bomber role. Hundreds of DH.4s were ordered for this purpose but hardly had this been done when a faster, long range day bomber was proposed as a redesign of the DH.4 to be called the DH.9.

The orders for the day bomber mildly-modified version of the DH.4 were cancelled and transferred to the DH.9 instead, but the Siddeley Puma engine for the DH.9 would have to develop 300 h.p. to out-perform the DH.4 as promised. At the moment when the contracts were amended in favour of the DH.9, the Puma was developing only 230 h.p. and was in deep trouble which practically stopped production. By the time the problems were solved in the Spring of 1918, the engine was still down in power and obsolete.

A second string to the bow was no less unfortunate: one thousand Fiat A.12 engines were also ordered for the DH.9 in 1917. It was a little more powerful than the Puma with 260 h.p. but would not have allowed the DH.9 to out perform the DH.4 as planned. In the event, they were too late. When the date arrived by which the 1000 engines should have been delivered, less than 60 had been received.

The lack of speed and low ceiling were a great handicap but the R.A.F. did their best with them. Lack of performance was not the only blight on what was basically a good airframe, as the engine proved unreliable and caused many missions to be aborted.

Armament—One Vickers gun synchronised to fire through the propeller, one Lewis gun on Scarff mounting ring in rear cockpit, 2 × 230 lb bombs stowed internally or under the fuselage or wings.

Performance—Max. speed at 15,000 ft with 2 × 230 lb bombs: 97·5 m.p.h. Climb to 15,000 ft with 2 × 230 lb bombs: 45 min. Service ceiling: 15,500 ft.

RE.8

The R.E.8 powered by the R.A.F.4a engine of 140 h.p. was known as the Harry Tate and might have been as funny as the famous comedian had it not been a dismal disappointment. It was designed as a replacement for the BE.2 series of reconnaissance aircraft. The BE two-seaters were very slow, virtually unarmed and the antithesis of manoeuvreable. The last characteristic resulted from the pre-1914 ideal that aeroplanes should be 'automatically stable' because the crashes and fatalities which accompanied the first flights of new types highlighted the difficulties with aeroplanes which were unstable. It must be mentioned in passing that designs of the day were little better than ideas, empirically translated with only a limited supply of materials; the designer/pilot often had to learn to fly on his first test flight.

The specification for the BE two-seater replacement stressed that it should be able to defend itself, and though manoeuvreability was not called for, it seems likely that the Factory would have been aware of the value of this attribute. In the event, the pilot of the RE.8 was designed into the front cockpit (he had been behind in the BE two-seaters) and given a synchronised machine gun; the observer behind him had a moveable Lewis gun. Unfortunately, the RE.8 was automatically stable.

Deliveries to Squadrons began in the last half of 1916 and were accompanied by a spate of accidents, many the results of spins with the virtual certainty that a nose-over on landing would cause the aircraft to go up in flames. The original drawings showed a large fin, but on the production aircraft this was reduced to a size less than the BE.2. This had a direct effect on spins and recovery from them. They tended to lose speed rapidly on the approach and observers were warned not to stand up to watch over the pilot's shoulder while landing—the extra drag caused the aeroplane to fall out of the sky. It earned a reputation as a bad and dangerous aircraft. Thousands were made.

By mid-1917 over 800 RE.8s had been supplied to squadrons to replace the BE two-seaters but the RE.8 offered no better chance of survival for the crews who had to fly them.

Armament—1 synchronised Vickers gun plus a Lewis gun in the rear cockpit. Bomb load 2 × 112 lb or 4 × 65 lb on racks under fuselage and wings.

Performance—Max. speed at 10,000 ft: without bombs, 96·5 m.p.h.; with 2 × 112 lb bombs 92·5 m.p.h. Climb to 10,000 ft: without bombs, 29 min; with 2 × 112 lb bombs 40 min.

A
3186

Hanriot HD.1

RenéHanriot designed and made his first aeroplane in 1907. In 1910 he had his own flying school and built several more of his monoplanes. In 1911 he started a flying school in England, at Brooklands. Soon afterwards, the Nieuport designer Pagny joined Hanriot and 2 two-seater monoplanes of Pagny design competed in the British Military Trials of 1912. Although they did not win, they were probably the best aircraft there.

Hanriot left his Company in 1913 but the business continued and their entry in the September 1913, Gordon Bennett Race was a little biplane with a 160 h.p. Gnome engine. This came second and reached a speed of 123 m.p.h.

In 1914 they produced a small biplane scout with a 50 h.p. Gnome, but it did not interest the authorities. Next they came out with the M.1. single seater fighter with the 80 h.p. le Rhone engine with a Lewis gun on the top centre section. It was tested by the famous Ace, Nungesser, but it crashed soon after take off and Nungesser was seriously injured.

That finished French interest in the M.1., but the Belgians were unable to get the Nieuports they wanted, so they ordered 30 modified M.1s redesigned after the crash with a long fin and enlarged tail plane. Unfortunately, the aircraft were still useless and were quickly withdrawn.

In the meantime, Rene Hanriot had re-entered the industry and was a major sub-contractor for the Sopwith 1½ Strutters built in France. With his designer Dupont he concocted the neat little single-seater HD.1 fighter with the 110 h.p. le Rhone engine. It had something of a Sopwith look about it and many constructional details were similar, as was to be expected. An individual feature of the HD.1 was the pronounced dihedral of the upper wing and its mounting so that the trailing edge was on a level with the pilot's eyes, so the view forward and upward was good.

The HD.1 was very manoeuvreable and had a performance similar to the Nieuport 17 (they had similar engines) but the Hanriot was overshadowed by the S.P.A.D. which became operational at the same time and replaced the Nieuport 17 in service.

However, the HD.1 was adopted by the Italians and made in Italy under licence. The Italians preferred it to the Nieuport 17 for its climbing ability, ease of handling and light controls.

Over 800 were delivered to the Italians, but the only users on the Western Front—the Belgians—received just over 100.

Armament—One synchronised Vickers machine gun (7 mm). A few had twin Vickers guns. Famous Belgian Ace Willy Coppens had a large bore Vickers gun (11 mm).

Performance—Max. speed at 10,000 ft: 101 m.p.h. Climb to 10,000 ft: 9 min.

Pfalz D.III

Pfalz was one of the factories which received a captured Nieuport 17 for study after the Types 11 and 17 had shown their superiority over the German fighters in 1916. So it was natural that a certain Nieuport flavour could be detected in the prototype Pfalz D.III when it began test flying early in 1917. In fact the resemblance was perhaps more superficial than any other of the Nieuport inspired German fighter types, because the construction was quite different.

As can be seen from the difference in the base of the wing V-struts Pfalz used two spars in the lower wing, instead of the one used in the Nieuport—the weak point in the design. Albatros used the single spar on their D.III and D.IV and duly ran into lower wing trouble.

The Pfalz performed well and was ordered into service; 276 were delivered by the end of 1917, probably about 1000 were built altogether.

The construction of the fuselage was complicated and was not so well suited to large production as the Albatros, or Fokker with its welded tube construction. It was a plywood shell—a semi stressed skin of very thin plywood strips wrapped around a light structure of spruce longerons on oval plywood formers. The ply strips were laid on at 45° to the fuselage centre line; there were two layers of strips, the second being at 90° to the first. The two layers were glued and finally reinforced with doped fabric.

The engine was the reliable 160 h.p. Mercedes and later the Pfalz D.IIIas had the up-rated 170/185 h.p. engine.

Armament—2 fixed Spandau machine guns firing through the propeller each with 500 rounds.

Performance—Max. speed at 10,000 ft: 102 m.p.h. Climb to 10,000 ft: 12 min.

PFALZ SCOUT.

Sopwith Triplane

Preceding the Triplane was the Sopwith Pup, also designed by Herbert Smith. It was entirely conventional but was considered one of the world's great aircraft because of its unrivalled handling and feel of harmony in flight which endeared the Pup to all who flew it.

The fuselage and tail assembly of the Triplane were similar to the Pup, though the Triplane had the advantage of an adjustable tail plane. The wings were of the same span as the Pup but of only 39 in chord, so that the total wing area came out a little less than the Pup. Each wing was built on two spars and there was an aileron on each wing. The struts were unusual being single members of wide chord, and the centre section struts picked up directly on both upper and lower longerons. The engine was at first the 110 h.p. Clerget 9Z but the 130 h.p. Clerget 9b was fitted to most aircraft used in Squadron Service.

They were first ordered by the Admiralty and joined the R.N.A.S. in France in June 1916. Only 150 or so were made because the initial orders were cut back, probably because the War Office had planned very large production of the Camel and this was beginning to show fruit.

The excellent rate of climb and manoeuvreability of the Triplane made it a match for the Albatros D.III and D.V. and it was considered by von Richthofen to be the best Allied fighter from early to mid-1917. The handling had been improved early in the year by the fitting of smaller elevators and tail plane.

Replacement of Triplanes with R.F.C. Squadrons by the Camel began in the summer of 1917 and it must have been one of the very few aircraft of its day which was superseded on the Western Front without being outclassed.

Armament—1 synchronised Vickers machine gun with 500 rounds (a few had twin Vickers).

Performance—Max. speed at 10,000 ft: 110 m.p.h. Climb to 10,000 ft: 11 min.

Sopwith Camel F.I

In 1916 the DH.2 and FE.2b had been able to combat the Fokker monoplanes, but the arrival in September 1916 of the Albatros D.I with two synchronised guns, followed by the D.II gave the advantage in air fighting to the Germans. The Sopwith Pup and Triplane held the balance for a few months, but a faster and more heavily armed fighter was needed.

The Camel was a descendant of the Pup and had two Vickers guns partly covered by a 'hump' on the top cowling behind the engine. The airframe was built entirely of wood. It was ordered for the R.F.C. with the 130 h.p. Clerget rotary engine, and for the R.N.A.S. with the 150 h.p. Bentley B.R.1 rotary. The latter was designed by Lt. W. O. Bentley and was the first aircooled engine to have aluminium cylinders.

Some Camels had the 110 h.p. Le Rhone rotary with which it was a little slower but climbed better. It was not easy to fly, like the Pup, 1½ strutter and Triplane. Wing Commander Norman McMillan wrote of it in his book *Into the blue*. "Here was a buzzing hornet, a wild thing burning the air like raw spirit fires the throat." It's powerful controls, the mass of engine, fuel, pilot and guns were concentrated close to the centre of gravity and the torque reaction of the engine (tending to turn the aeroplane round the propeller shaft) could quickly transform a turn into a spin without warning. This could be used to advantage by an experienced pilot, but unfortunately many were killed by spinning before they gained the necessary experience. The extraordinary manoeuvreability of the Camel enabled it to hold its own to the end of the War. 1325 Camels were produced in 1917 and a further 500 were ordered at the end of that year.

There was a Night Fighter version for Home Defence against the German bombers. The Vickers guns were removed so that the pilot should not be blinded by their flash when firing, and also because it was thought undesirable to fire incendiary bullets through the propeller. Two Lewis guns were mounted on the top wing. The pilots cockpit was moved back to get a better view upwards and the seat raised.

Armament—In addition to the guns mentioned for Day and Night fighter versions, 4 × 20 lb bombs could be carried on racks under the fuselage.

N6332

Nieuport 17

Capt. Bishop was posted to No. 11 Squadron R.F.C. in May 1916 to fly the new Nieuport 17. He shot down his first two German aircraft before the end of the month. Before his death, just a year later, his confirmed score was 44, most of them shot down using his famous B.1566. Latterly he alternated use of the Nieuport with an SE.5 as these were replacing the Nieuport 17 in British Squadrons.

A feature of the British Nieuports was the Lewis gun mounting modification carried out by Sergeant Foster of No. 11 Squadron. He altered the mounting so that the gun could be pulled down to a 45° position to fire upwards into the belly of enemy aircraft while the Nieuport passed underneath. This method of attack was at first the speciality of Capt. Ball. During a visit to Farnborough, Ball made several suggestions for the improvement of the SE.5 which was then coming off the production line. The use of this type of gun mounting was one of them. With Guynemer as his opposite number on the French side, Ball was the spearhead of the British swing to air mastery in 1916, after the bad days of 1915 and the 'Fokker Menace'.

The Type 17 was the most famous of the family and was much copied by the Germans, who supplied captured specimens to Albatros, Fokker, Pfalz and other manufacturers. The sesquiplane layout was adopted mainly to obtain the benefit of the low drag of the monoplane wing with the strength of the easily-stressed 'bridge' structure of the biplane. It also proved to have an aerodynamic advantage over the conventional biplane arrangement as the larger gap between upper and lower wings reduced interference and improved the lift/drag ratio.

Fuselage construction was of steel tubes in the front section, while the rear was a wire braced, fabric covered, wooden structure. The upper wing had two spars, the front very close to the leading edge, the rear spar being vertically over the single spar of the lower wing. This proved to be the weak point in the design of the Type 11 Bebe and some failures occurred and lower wings broke or fell off. The Type 17 was strengthened in this area, although static tests did not reveal any weakness in the spar of the lower wing. It was some time before it was realised that it was not lack of ultimate strength which caused the failures, but the twisting movement about the lower wing due to the spar being too far back, which caused the lower wings to break.

Performance—Max. speed: 107 m.p.h. at 6500 ft; 101 m.p.h. at 10,000 ft. Climb: $5\frac{1}{2}$ min to 6500 ft; 9 min to 10,000 ft.

B1566

Fokker Triplane DR.1

Early in 1917 the R.N.A.S. Sopwith Triplanes shocked the Germans with their terrific rate of climb and unexcelled manoeuvreability. The state of the art of fighter design at that time was such that the Germans may have believed that the triplane was the ultimate.

However that may be, the German Air Ministry wrote in July 1917 to all German and Austrian constructors and asked them to build experimental triplane fighters for evaluation. More than a dozen makers responded. (Little did they know that the British had already started on the design of the Camel, which was to eclipse the triplane).

Fokker was accustomed to visit the front fairly frequently and in April 1917 he heard at first hand from von Richthofen about the remarkable Sopwith Triplane—possibly he was told of the occasion when one lone Triplane attacked eleven Albatros D.IIIs, outmanoeuvred them all and escaped scot free.

Fokker was duly impressed and thus had a head start with his Chief Designer Platz in the design of a triplane of his own powered by a rotary engine.

Platz did not copy the Sopwith Triplane—he probably never saw one—bu followed his previous design philosophy. His triplane had cantilever wings with two box spars and no external bracing wires. As before, the fuselage was of welded steel tubes.

Fokker carried out the flight testing and made several improvements. The rotary engines were at first very good Swedish copies of the 110 h.p. le Rhone, but when that supply dried up, they came from the Oberursel factory in which Fokker had recently obtained an interest.

The Fokker Triplane offers a good example of the speed with which the Germans—and Fokker in particular—transferred the design of an aircraft from a chalked layout on the floor to a reality in Squadron service. From an idea in April through prototype construction, and test flying leading to an initial order in July for 320 aircraft, it took only five weeks more to get a few into action in late August: a total of only five months.

There may have been too much haste, as the DR.1 Triplanes were grounded in November after the wings of two of them broke up in flight. This was due to bad workmanship and faulty assembly. Some modifications were made and sound new wings fitted to all triplanes and they were back in service within a month. All this upset the production programme, so that only 30 were delivered by the end of November instead of the 170 which had been planned.

Although the rate of climb and manoeuvreability were outstanding, the Fokker Triplane was not fast enough to catch a DH.4, DH.9 or Bristol fighter. The Triplanes continued in service until May 1918 when they were replaced by the Fokker D.VII.

Armament—2 fixed synchronised LMG.08/15 machine guns with 1000 rounds.

Performance—Max. speed at 13,000 ft: 102 m.p.h. Climb to 13,000 ft: 15 min.

FOKKER TRIPLANE.

SE.5a

The forerunner of the SE.5a was the SE.5 which came into service in France in April 1917. Produced by the Royal Aircraft Factory, it was designed by H. P. Folland. It had a Hispano Suiza 150 h.p. V-8 engine.

It had always been intended to fit the 200 h.p. geared Hispano Suiza engine as soon as it became available. The Admiralty had the foresight to order 8000 of these late in 1916, but engines from this order did not become available until early 1918.

The SE.5a was a cleaned up and modified version of the SE.5 following testing and squadron experience and reports. It too suffered delays because the 200 h.p. engines were not ready; the engine supply situation was so bad that in early 1918 there were 400 SE.5as waiting for engines. The troubles were concerned with crankshafts breaking and reduction gears failing. One French sub-contractor's reduction gears regularly failed after a 'life' of only 4 hours, but were nevertheless accepted as better than no gears at all.

Wolseley's were making the 200 h.p. engine also, and were likewise in trouble with it. But they also re-designed the 150 h.p. engine as the Wolseley Viper eventually developed to give 200 h.p. From April 1917 these were fitted in several hundred SE.5as when no 200 h.p. engines were available.

Armament—One synchronised Vickers gun with 400 rounds. One Lewis gun on the top wing with 4 drums each holding 97 rounds. The gun had to be pulled back down to the cockpit to change drums, an awkward task.

Performance—Max. speed m.p.h. (200 h.p. engine): 130 at 10,000 ft. Climb to 10,000 ft: 11 min.

B4897
LIFT HERE

Bristol Fighter F.2B

Late in 1915 the R.F.C. drew up a specification for the reconnaissance aircraft they needed. Essentially it had to be able to defend itself. The Royal Aircraft Factory produced the RE.8 to meet this need and thousands of this unsatisfactory type were built.

At the same time, Bristol designer Barnwell also started scheming out a BE.2 replacement. Various engines were considered in preliminary designs but when the prototype appeared in late 1916 as the F.2A, it had a 190 h.p. Rolls Royce Falcon engine and a machine gun firing through the propeller, with another gun on a ring mounting in the rear cockpit.

Fifty of these F.2As were delivered and first used in the Battle of Arras in April 1917. They did not have an auspicious start and losses were heavy. It is just possible that some reconnaissance pilots did not fully appreciate and make full use of the F.2A's potential as a fighting aircraft.

There were some pilots, however, who flung the Bristol about just like any fighter of that day, using the front gun for attack and depending on the observer to use his gun to guard their rear. These tactics were very successful and started the aircraft on its long and popular career.

The next 200 Bristol Fighters were known as F.2B, as some modifications including certain fuselage and wing attachment improvements had been made in this batch. The last 50 of these had the Rolls Royce Falcon II engine of 275 h.p. and it is this version of the F.2B which really earned its great reputation.

Hundreds more were ordered and built but in late 1917 the production of Falcons was quite insufficient; only the Bristol-built F.2Bs continued to have Falcon engines. The aircraft made by other sub-contractors were variously fitted with Sunbeam Arab and Siddeley Puma engines. Neither engine was very good and certainly not in the class of the Falcon. At the end of the war, the R.A.F. had over 700, Arab-powered, Bristol Fighters but only 80 were in action in France.

The constructional characteristic which immediately identified the Bristol Fighter was the mounting of the fuselage in mid-gap between the wings. The continuation of the lower wing lifting surface uninterrupted below the fuselage was an aerodynamic advantage.

The F.2B continued with the R.A.F. in service well into the 1920s and was widely used by foreign air forces.

Armament—One synchronised Vickers firing through the propeller; one or two Lewis on Scarff ring mounting in rear cockpit.

Performance—Max. speed at 10,000 ft: 111 m.p.h. Climb to 10,000 ft: 13 min.

J·6790
J
6790

Breguet 14B2

At the time Louis Breguet began working on the design of his type 14 in mid-1916, the authorities were only just weakening in their resolve to have nothing but pusher aircraft for military use. Breguet also had to overcome their other misgivings about it. Firstly, they wanted to install the 200 h.p. Hispano Suiza engine and secondly, they had doubts about its unusual construction.

The fuselage employed dural longerons and cross members bolted together with welded steel fittings—probably the first use of duralumin in this way. The main spars of the wings were rectangular dural tubes with wooden ribs. All the tail surfaces were of welded steel tubing.

There was a rectangular radiator in front of the 12-cylinder Renault engine (then of 220 h.p.) which Breguet insisted on using, as he had done in his Type 5. The slab sided multi-louvred engine cowling, slight back stagger and sweep back of the main planes and the sturdy undercarriage made it eye-catching but not a thing of beauty.

More than 2000 Type 14 were ordered during 1917 in two versions—A2 for reconnaissance with a camera, wireless transmitter and racks for 4 × 120 mm bombs, and the B2 bomber which had extended lower wings with Michelin bomb racks which could carry 32 × 115 mm bombs or an equivalent load of other sizes of bomb. The B2 had a window in the side of the fuselage and both pilot and observer had trapdoors in the floor to give a good view of the ground. Both A2 and B2 had dual controls. The B2 had trailing edge flaps which blew up by wind pressure at 70 m.p.h. but extended themselves automatically for landing and take off.

By the time both variants appeared in the summer of 1917, the Renault 12 was giving 300 h.p. Both A2 and B2 were used to re-equip squadrons which had been using Sopwith 1½ Strutters. Many of the B2s on ground support duties were furnished with armoured seats and some had a Lewis gun firing downwards and rearwards under the fuselage.

Like the Bristol Fighter, the Breguet 14B2 had a long history and when production ceased, in 1926, at least 8000 had been made.

Armament—1 fixed Vickers synchronised gun on top of the fuselage, sometimes replaced or augmented by a Lewis gun on the top of the centre section. The observer had twin Lewis guns on a ring mounting and sometimes a rearward and downward firing Lewis as well.

Performance—Max. speed at 10,000 ft: 107 m.p.h. Climb to 10,000 ft: 11½ min.

Albatros D.V.

In 1917 the Albatros D.V. became the principal type used by the Jastas formed in 1916. It was a logical development of its forerunner the D.IV but with sesquiplane wings like the Nieuport 17. It was lighter than the D.IV and although at first it has the same engine, the Mercedes D.III 160 h.p., it later had the 180/185 h.p. engine.

It performed well against the Allies, Camels, SE.5s and Spads, but did not establish any ascendancy over them.

The fuselage had much the same sleek look and good finish as the Pfalz D.III but was made in a simpler manner and was more suited to large production. Instead of the complicated wrap-around strips, ply panels were pinned, screwed and glued onto eight longerons supported on ply formers which changed in section from circular at the front to nearly knife-edge at the tail.

Some thousands were made and from January to May 1918 there were between 700 and 1000 in action on the Western Front.

The single spar construction of the lower wing led (as with the Nieuport) to some failures in the air and all Albatros D.V. pilots were warned against excessive speeds in the dive.

Armament—Two Spandau machine guns firing through the propeller.

Performance—Max. speed: 103 m.p.h. Climb to 10,000 ft: 15 min.

ALBATROS SCOUT. D. 5.

Fokker D.VII

The Fokker D.VII design won from thirty rivals an official competition in Berlin in January 1918, for a single-seater fighter using the 160 h.p. Mercedes engine. 400 were ordered immediately, using the triplane fuselage and tail to speed production. The rival Albatros factory was also ordered to make D.VII at a cheaper price than that paid to Fokker, since they had no development expenses to meet. Fokker also received a royalty on each Albatros version.

Designed by Platz, who had been with Fokker from the beginning as a welding specialist, it was the first operational German aircraft to use a car-type honeycomb radiator in the nose. The fuselage was of welded tube. The wing was built on two wooden box spars with a 3-ply leading edge. The scalloped trailing edge resulted from it being formed on a wire stretched through eyelets at the tip of the ribs. The lower wing was narrower than the upper (to improve downward view) and the struts were of steel; there were no bracing wires. The whole aircraft was fabric covered except for the metal nose panels.

The second version, fitted with a B.M.W. engine, provided power above 18,000 ft and since good manoeuvreability was retained at such heights, it was superior to all adversaries.

Armament—2 fixed synchronised Spandau machine guns firing forwards, each with 500 rounds.

Performance—Max speed m.p.h.: Mercedes 118; B.M.W. 125. Climb: 16,000 ft in 19 min; 20,000 ft in 38 min.

Spad XIII

Bechereau was the designer of the pre-war Deperdussin aircraft and remained with the Company when it was reorganised into S.P.A.D. by Louis Bleriot in 1914, after Deperdussin himself got into financial difficulties with some scandal attached.

Bechereau thought that rotary engines would soon reach the limit of their power development and that future fighters should be built around water cooled engines. The Germans were of much the same opinion and developed their Mercedes and Benz water cooled, in-line engines, born of pre-war Grand Prix motor racing experience.

In 1915, a new, liquid-cooled engine was being tested and evaluated in both France and England. This was the Hispano Suiza V-eight, the product of a Spanish motor car factory in the Rolls Royce class, designed by a Swiss engineer, Birkigt. The aero engine was made in France and eventually made under licence by sub-contractors in many countries. Bechereau designed the Spad VII around it, and the Royal Aircraft Factory did likewise with the SE.5.

The engine was very light for its power and competitive with the air cooled rotaries. It produced 220 h.p. The Spad VII went into service with it in late 1916. It was followed by the Spad XIII about a year later. There is no doubt that the Spad XIII together with the SE.5a, available in large numbers on the Western Front in 1918, had command of the air and exerted a considerable influence on the result of the war.

There were troubles with the French built Hispano Suiza reduction gears, but the designer stayed with the geared engine and eventually it earned a good reputation for reliability in the Spad XIII.

The aircraft had a conventional fuselage formed on a square section, wire braced, wood girder and the wings were built on box section spars. The trailing edges of wire stretched along the tail ends of the ribs imparted the usual French scalloped effect. It was, in fact, a single bay biplane but, from a little distance, appeared to have two bays each side. This was because tie-struts were fitted at half span to prevent the bracing wires whipping and chafing.

It was a very strong aircraft and in high speed dives it was never the Spad XIII wings which broke up or fell off.

Armament—Two synchronised Vickers machine guns. (There was a later version with a cannon firing through the propeller boss of the geared engine.)

Performance—Max speed at 10,000 ft: 133 m.p.h. Climb to 10,000 ft: 8 min.

Ansaldo SVA.5

Until 1916, the Caproni bombers were the principal examples of native Italian design. Most of the aircraft built in Italy were to foreign designs, many being French.

Then two Engineer Officers of the Military Aviation Technical Directorate collaborated with two civilian engineers to design a fighter. The Italian Government financed the giant engineering firm of Ansaldo to build a new factory to produce the new SVA fighter. The initials stood for Savoia and Verduzio (the two Engineer Officers) and Ansaldo. It was intended to complete on level terms with the fastest fighters of the time and in addition be capable of long range. The prototype flew early in 1917.

It was several miles per hour faster than any aircraft on the Italian front and owed its speed to the care taken to achieve it in the design. The wings were of thin section and the trailing edge deflected upward a little at speed, reducing drag; at low speeds there was almost a flap effect giving more lift for landing and take-off. The wings were braced by a Warren girder between the struts. The fuselage was a simple spruce structure covered with ply panels, but with the unusual feature that behind the cockpit the usual four longerons were arranged to fair into three, two upper and one lower, giving a triangular cross-section behind the cockpit. This led to an improved form, saved weight and probably improved the effectiveness of the tail surfaces for a given size.

The engine was the reliable S.P.A.6A of 205 h.p. which later developed 220 h.p. The performance of the SVA.5 was so good that it could function as a reconnaissance aircraft without escort, take on any enemy fighter and, if necessary when outnumbered, climb away at high speed. In service early in 1918, it was used mainly for reconnaissance and as a light bomber to carry out strategic bombing missions involving flights of 400 to 600 miles—exceptional ranges for that time.

Over 1200 were built and played a large part in achieving superiority for the Italians over the Austro-Hungarian forces opposing them.

Armament—Two synchronised Vickers machine guns.

Performance—max speed: 143 m.p.h. Climb to 10,000 ft: 10 min.